The Solo Performer's Journey

From the Page to the Stage

Michael Kearns

HEINEMANN
Portsmouth, NH

Heinemann
A division of Reed Elsevier Inc.
361 Hanover Street
Portsmouth, NH 03801–3912
www.heinemanndrama.com

Offices and agents throughout the world

Library of Congress Cataloging-in-Publication Data
Kearns, Michael, 1950–
     The solo performer's journey : from the page to the stage / Michael Kearns.
        p. cm.
     ISBN 0-325-00752-7 (alk. paper)
1. One-person shows (performing arts). 2. Monodramas—History and criticism.
3. Playwriting. I. Title.

PN1936.K43 2005
791—dc22   2004030685

Editor: Lisa A. Barnett
Production: Vicki Kasabian
Cover design: Catherine Hawkes/Cat & Mouse
Compositor: Reuben Kantor, QEP Design
Manufacturing: Louise Richardson

Printed in the United States of America on acid-free paper
09 08 07 06 05 DA 1 2 3 4 5

Contents

Acknowledgments

To suggest that only one person creates a solo performance piece would be as ludicrous as saying that one person is entirely responsible for the publication of a book.

There would be no *Solo Performer's Journey* without editor Lisa Barnett's invaluable input, marking our fourth collaboration. For whatever reason, this outing seemed cozier even though we were separated by a couple of thousand miles. It really felt like we were working side by side.

With Lisa, it's a role-reversal position to my work with Precious. In addition to editor, Lisa plays director, therapist, confidante, and savior. Always with good humor and almost always making criticism bearable, she guides the project, acting as the continuity person, the arbiter of good taste, as well as the one who preserves my image.

Working with Lisa, even from afar, had the same levels of intimacy and intensity I experienced with Precious. I consider myself blessed to be in the company of these kick-ass women who, personally and professionally, offer me ideas and advice, love and support while always teaching me the true meaning of work ethic and professionalism. I dedicate *The Solo Performer's Journey* to Precious Chong and Lisa Barnett.

There are other spectacular artists and friends who lent their seasoned voices to these pages: Tim Miller, Jenny Sullivan, Dan Kwong, Mark Travis, Danielle Brazell, Mary Milelzcik, David Nichols, Alec Mapa, Syd Rushing, Seth Cutler, Melanie DuPuy, Rob Sullivan, Harry Hart Browne, Gary Guidinger, Linda Toliver, Irene Pinn, and Harris Smith.

On a personal note, there are my trusted friends (you know who you are) and members of the Kearns' extended family who make it possible for me to pursue an artistic life in tandem with life as a single parent.

Finally, there is Tia Katherine Kearns—the reason why my real life is a duet and not a solo.

Introduction

It has been said that we enter this world and exit this world alone. And many of us spend much of our lives alone on a stage, attempting to make sense of what happens to us in between that entrance and exit, between birth and death.

Michael Kearns, *Getting Your Solo Act Together*

The blank page and the empty stage beckon. Your heartbeat accelerates at the thought of facing either, yet there will be no solo performance in your future unless you surrender to both. Do the page and the stage call out your name?

If you decide to face the page and the stage, it will be like entering a relationship. A relationship that will propel you to euphoric heights but also drop you to hellish depths. A love-hate relationship, in fact, and one that you might want to walk away from on more than one occasion.

The process that transports you from the first words you write on the page to the first steps you take on the stage will frustrate you, scare you, empower you, irritate you, and educate you. But if you embark on a solo journey, you just might be giving yourself a ticket to artistic viability.

As an actor who wrote (mostly journalism) and/or a writer who acted, I never felt like I was making art. It was only after my second solo show, *intimacies,* that I dared to call myself an artist (and it had nothing to do with that "performance artist" label).

Not only have I taken this solo trip several times, but I've been lucky enough to go along for the ride with several other adventurous souls. And I've got stories to tell.

As scary as it is seductive, the road to a solo performance must be carefully planned. My first book on the subject, *Getting Your Solo Act*

Together (Heinemann, 1997), was a nuts-and-bolts approach. *The Solo Performer's Journey: From the Page to the Stage* more closely resembles what solo performance does. This book tells stories. Interspersed with practical suggestions, personal stories, advice, and some warnings, *The Solo Performer's Journey* tracks the two-year excursion of Precious Chong's *Porcelain Penelope Shows.*

How many people have you heard announce that they are planning "to do a solo show"? Very few of these dream shows make it to the page, and fewer still make it to the stage. The reason? It's a four-letter word: w-o-r-k. I couldn't begin to estimate the number of hours—over a two-year period—that Precious spent writing and rewriting, rehearsing, schlepping costumes and props, and trying to drum up audiences.

It's been one helluva ride—from our initial meeting to a run in New York—and I hope you hop on for the trip. Almost every aspect of solo is addressed as we move from one version of the show to another, from one theatre to another, from one city to another, from one drummer to another, from one personal upheaval to another.

For the purposes of this book, I concentrate on shows that are written and performed by the same artist. These shows usually fall into two categories: fiction or nonfiction (even though definitions can be stretched). Lily Tomlin would fall into the fiction category while the late Spalding Gray was decidedly a nonfiction solo artist.

One of the first one-man performances I saw was Rob Sullivan's *Flower Ladies and Pistol Kids* in 1981, a simple evening of vivid storytelling superbly written and performed. I had no choice—I was compelled to create one!

I honestly thought that I had gotten the "written and performed by" piece out of my system when I did *The Truth Is Bad Enough* in 1983. Interestingly enough, when Tim Miller first saw me work solo (in the late '80s) it was in a one-man play (*Dream Man*, written by James Carroll Pickett). Based on his familiarity with my work as a journalist and the performance he saw that night, Tim strongly suggested that I write a piece for myself. I did, and that work, *intimacies,* launched what has become a career largely defined by solo work. Thank you, Timmy.

Beginning with *intimacies* in 1989, one show followed another, and then I began directing and producing solo work. This form has never ceased to exhilarate me. When it works, there is nothing more challenging to create or riveting to experience.

The solo form has also given me the freedom to connect to stories—my own and others'—that is often not acceptable in other entertainment forms. Censorship is virtually nonexistent in this work, and I find I can bring to life and to the stage the most intimate narratives and nuanced performances that might not fly elsewhere.

I wrote *Getting Your Solo Act Together* as a response to aspiring performers who had the instincts to create a one-person show but not the tools. Because of the book's positive response, I decided to do a solo lab but I didn't want to do it alone. (There's a joke there.) I enlisted the help of Rob Sullivan, one of my solo heroes and a friend of more than twenty years. The lab, like this book, primarily concentrated on "written and performed by" pieces, but we would consider other forms of solo. If, for example, someone who was writing a one-hander for an actor to perform (in the tradition of Julie Harris' seminal *Belle of Amherst,* written by William Luce), we'd sign them up.

Many permutations of solo performance have evolved over the years and bastardizations of the form have escalated as a result of America's obsession with stardom; from reality TV to rants, everyone wants their five minutes of fame. Sadly, the solo show often becomes the playing field of choice that provides the short-lived spotlight.

There is no strict definition for this genre. In some instances, a nightclub act could be considered a solo performance (especially if it contains a considerable amount of monologue material). Certainly Elaine Stritch's Tony Award–winning *Elaine Stritch at Liberty* is solo at its best, even though she employs song lyrics that she didn't write.

What I don't, however, consider "solo performance" includes book readings (even if they are acted out), poetry readings (even if they're brilliant), karaoke (God help us), and rants, raves, slams, or whatever other excuses devised for star-struck wannabes to get in front of an audience. Solo performance is an art, not a hobby.

If you believe the six degrees of separation theory, there are probably only three degrees of separation in the world of the theatre (and maybe two degrees in the more intimately connected field of solo). This is a story that confirms my personal thesis: the story of Jenny and Precious and Michael.

Jenny Sullivan (no relation to Rob) had directed me in a play after she saw me do *intimacies* at the University of Santa Barbara. She remembers telling people after that performance that she wanted to work with me if she ever decided to do a solo performance piece.

Jenny joined the lab that Rob and I conducted and immediately proved to be one of our most industrious and ingenious students. The daughter of actor Barry Sullivan, Jenny was dealing with enduring roller-coaster relationships with her deceased father and her very much alive mentally retarded brother, John.

From the first session, Jenny expressed doubt as to whether the story she wanted to tell would best be served by the solo format. She was, however, clearly stimulated by the class, and tackled the achingly personal yet unquestionably universal theme of a daughter who felt eclipsed by her father's larger-than-life persona and his dedication to his troubled son. In spite of her worries about the format, I steered the piece as if it was going to be a one-woman performance piece.

While Rob and I provided feedback to all of our students, we concentrated on the stories we felt we best grasped. Jenny's became my baby.

Only in retrospect do I ever question what draws me to a particular piece. It either speaks to me or it doesn't (and if it doesn't, I would never consider signing on as a director). I could teach someone who was creating work that didn't inspire me but I couldn't attach my name as director unless there was a level of passion. It wouldn't be fair to either of us.

When a project moves from the classroom into a theatre and I switch roles from teacher to director, a host of questions arise, some of which are unfounded and based on my own insecurities. In this particular instance, I was certain some critic would say that Jenny's show should be directed by a woman. I still didn't really get it. Why did I feel I was the perfect man for the job?

Jenny wrote autobiographical monologues with heart-tugging conviction but, like so many performers who dare to go solo, she felt self-indulgent, embarrassed, and unworthy of telling the story in the first person even though how she felt had nothing to do with the reality: she had a compelling story to tell and the physical and vocal prowess to engage an audience on her own.

In *Getting Your Solo Act Together, Los Angeles Times* theatre critic Kathleen Foley makes some excellent points:

> If you are performing autobiographical work, universality
> becomes even more essential. No matter how dramatic the
> details of your personal experience, they must translate
> beyond your circle to a wider audience. Of course, you can
> be shocking, abrasive, downbeat, or downright radical—as
> long as you are not boring. Constantly monitor your perfor-
> mance for any signs of personal egotism . . . And bear in
> mind that if you are at all self-righteous, politically exclu-
> sive—or, worst of all, self-pitying—you will invite failure.

I honestly can't say whether it was her reluctance to do a one-person show or the unraveling of her story that organically shifted it to being a three-character play. It doesn't matter. She found the best way to tell her story by putting her father and her brother on stage with her. The lesson here? The artist must, first and foremost, be comfortable with the form of her show or disaster will strike. Although not in the form she originally envisioned, Jenny's dream became a reality in *J for J,* and resulted in a number of full-scale productions.

Even though I wondered whether a woman director might be better for what was clearly a woman's story, I had continued to work with Jenny as a dramaturg during the process, from writing a solo piece to writing a three-character play. Then one day, like a neon sign flashing in my head, I realized why I was so close to her story.

The intense bond between father and daughter was the thread that tied Jenny's story to mine. While I'm not suggesting I achieved Barry Sullivan's track record as a film and television star, the dynamics of my relationship with my daughter, Tia, mirrored the Sullivans'. When Jenny talked about visiting her dad at his dressing room on the MGM lot, I would connect it to Tia's presence in theatre dressing rooms, coast to coast, from the time she was eight months old.

Precious Chong had worked with Jenny on a play and was among the many peers who attended *J for J* in its wildly successful run at LA's Court Theatre. Now this became a triangular relationship, made even more incestuous considering that Precious and Jenny had played two of my love interests in a film directed by Bill Haugse.

The bonds formed in these situations are often the result of uncommon intimacy and shared connections to family. And family ties—mothers, daughters, fathers, son, brothers, sisters—of course, are subjects that drive a large number of solo works. The father-daughter relationship is the recurring theme of the story that links Jenny and Precious and Michael.

Even though Jenny's show had evolved into a riveting play (with Jeff Kober as her father and John Ritter as her brother), Jenny kindly acknowledged the work she'd done with Rob and me, giving us an ad in her program.

Although Precious and I had some heavy-duty scenes in Bill's movie, including some uncompromising love scenes, our closeness hadn't extended beyond the shoot. So I was surprised to get a call from her, saying that she'd "seen the ad in Jenny's program" and wanted to meet about the possibility of doing a solo show.

Little did I realize that this would be the beginning of a professional and personal teaming that would not only endure but deepen over the next two years; a theatrical marriage where we eventually spoke in shorthand, finished each other's sentences, and honestly had no memory of who brought which brilliant (or terrible) idea to the table and sometimes to the stage.

Precious' story would reveal, I soon found out, the rich and complex relationship with her father, Tommy Chong. Again, as a potential director and a father, I could relate.

Now we shift to the story that drives *The Solo Performer's Journey.* It is, in addition to being a practical guide to solo performance, a memoir about my two-year teaming with Precious Chong and her cast of characters that comprised the series of *Porcelain Penelope Shows.*

We began our process trusting her talent and each other. Her energy, as both a writer and a performer, was boundless. We enjoyed powerful collaborations with other artists who were brought onto the project. When the going got tough (and it did), Precious summoned perseverance beyond the call of duty and had the necessary courage and stamina to allow the show to grow. Did all this hard work and diligence result in a Broadway run or a special on HBO? Not yet, but she found success.

By sharing the story of the ever-evolving *Porcelain Penelope Show,* I hope to inspire you, teach you, motivate you, amuse you (on occasion), and, yes, caution you. Not everyone possesses the skill, the drive, and the bravery of Precious Chong. Without question, *The Solo Performer's Journey: From the Page to Stage* is her story as well as mine.

Remember the journey from the page to the stage is not without perils but it promises the magic and discovery that only an artistic trip can offer.

I hope you enjoy the ride! All aboard!

1 Trust

Trust begins with your own process and ends with that of your audience.

David Nichols

She arrived at my apartment, as instructed, with several pages of notes stuffed into her oversized straw purse. She almost always wears a floppy, funky straw hat and cute sandals. That day was no exception. I was impressed that she actually brought two copies of her material since most performers forget this courtesy, even though I make that request during our pre-meeting phone call.

I looked at her differently now than I did when she was playing my kooky, neurotic love interest in the independent film we did together. While she possesses a certain childlike energy, it's apparent she's one smart cookie. She is also an undeniably but unconventionally beautiful creature—with almond-shaped eyes, red hair, and alabaster skin.

The first meeting I have with a prospective student is critical. It provides an opportunity for us to get a sense of each other and make the initial decision: whether to embark on what can evolve into an intense working relationship.

My request that the student bring something in writing ("two copies, please") is so that I can actually have something tangible in front of me. I stress that it does not have to be a formal proposal or outline. It can be scribbled notes, random ideas, a line or two, a few character names. Since I charge for this initial session (at least $75 for an hour), I want it to be valuable for both of us. I also want to determine the level of commitment. If someone cannot bring himself to put words on paper (whether it's done on a computer or written on napkins with lipstick, I don't care), he will probably never write a solo show.

Do people show up without anything in writing? You betcha, and they spout every line from that old standard ("my dog ate it") to self-important excuses ("I had sooo many auditions last week"). Rarely do we recover from this initial faux pas on the part of the potential student.

Overkill can also be a warning sign. One very ambitious actress brought in a notebook with at least two-hundred typewritten pages, detailing the life of a film star. (She was also dressed like her and, no, I'm not kidding.) Way too much information, thank you very much.

Precious brought in a few monologues, unpunctuated and badly spelled, on coffee-stained paper. It didn't matter. The words leapt off the page with specificity and strength. I knew she was a good actress and, after a quick look at those pages, I knew she was a good writer as well.

One of my goals during this first meeting is to assess (and sometimes I guess at) the performer's skills as a writer versus their skills as a performer. Is one stronger? Is one virtually nonexistent?

When Eugene Paulish (a veteran of my solo class) decided to put his piece (*But Stevie Nicks Understands*) on the boards, I knew I was dealing with a very talented writer with no stage experience. This is workable but we need to be on the same page in terms of the process we're going to use. If a mediocre actress wants to do the life of Sarah Bernhardt, I'd caution against it no matter how brilliant her script might be.

Precious had begun creating a number of characters in various classes and workshops she'd attended, but she wasn't certain how to string them together.

If you haven't given birth to your characters in a classroom or workshop situation (as Precious did), here's a bit of advice (from *Getting Your Solo Act Together*):

> Building a bio of your character(s) is imperative to establish a
> believable flesh-and-blood human being. Some things to con-

2

sider: birth date, place of birth, ethnicity, family roots, class standing, educational background, sexual history, physical characteristics, and mannerisms. I suggest writing the bio in the first person so you begin to meld with the character(s) you're creating.

Once I've established the degree of skills, the most important question is What do you want to say? "I genuinely believe that we all entered into this business as artists simply because we each felt we had something to say," Mark Travis says, "something to share. So we became writers, directors, actors, dancers, singers, etc. And all our lives we struggle to refine ourselves within our chosen discipline and we struggle to find and tell the stories we want to tell.

"Sadly, most actors are relegated to telling the stories of others, assisting others in their self-expression. But, once a performer chooses to go the solo route, everything changes. You get to write your own material. You get to perform it, deliver it to the audience, by yourself. It's pure. It can be, if you are courageous enough, purely and honestly and openly you.

"You can tell your story in any way you like. You can bring us through your experiences in such a way that we share the experience with you, have the same reactions, see it from your point of view. In other words, we get to be you for the evening. Wow."

It is not a test. There is no right or wrong answer and the final product almost never winds up being what one initially envisioned, but the soloist needs to have a point of view—even if it seems unclear, messy, conflicted, hackneyed, or sketchy.

Solo work has two cardinal rules. You must have something to say and you must have the skill to say it entertainingly. I'm not suggesting that every solo performer must possess John Leguizamo's timing or the literary prowess of Holly Hughes or Spalding Gray's unique take on the world or Tim Miller's physicality or Lily Tomlin's ability to switch from character to character.

What you do need is physical and vocal energy and a story that takes the audience on a ride. Note that I didn't say a story that teaches or informs or makes a political point or proves a thesis or puts down your ex or numbingly lets us know you're a victim of God knows what. I said, "A story that takes the audience on a ride" and by that I mean a story and a stage presence that entertain, enlighten, and ultimately move your audience.

If you trust your instincts, like Precious does, you'll be ahead of the game. Porcelain Penelope, who would be the headliner of her show, was "a character based on my wounded child," she said, that she had developed in her acting class a year prior.

The Hooligan, a macho Australian bloke, was "based on my astrological sign, Aries," she said, rolling her eyes. Also created in acting class, the Hooligan was a hedonist—crude, horny, and lascivious. The only other male character was Mr. H (as in "Hitler") who was an overbearing bully and woman-hater.

When Precious heard Temple Grandin being interviewed on NPR, she based a character on the autistic woman who, because "she thinks like an animal," is able to design slaughterhouses that protect animals from severe pain and trauma. Precious took threads of Grandin's story and created a fictitious character who is an unseen grip for her family's circus act and is determined to break free from the pressure of her family's visible success.

Writing a character in acting class "based on Christmas," Precious paid tribute to her Grandma, simply because she reminded her of Christmas. "I often go into the assignment sideways," she admitted. The Sexy Mom character, clearly showing her autobiographical roots, was birthed in the widely respected comedy-improv Groundlings class. The Grandma and the Sexy Mom characters were largely based on reality but written with poetic license.

Emma, the Stripper Who Talks, grew out of an audition for an independent movie. Precious wrote herself a monologue to perform for the director, based on a woman who has a sexual flirtation with her son. She wound up getting the film role and adding a viable character to her stable of performable misfits.

The Talking Vagina (who also sang) was a loudmouth who voiced things that good girls shouldn't say. The Snake Girl had not been written or conceived at this point, and we didn't know yet that Precious would eventually become a character in her own show.

We began with the following eight characters, in various stages of development: Porcelain Penelope, the Hooligan, Mr H, Temple, Grandma, the Sexy Mom, Emma, and the Vagina. During this initial meeting Precious and I also agreed on "new vaudeville" as a descriptive phrase to conceptualize *The Porcelain Penelope Show*. Even though her show was in an embryonic stage, Precious knew that *The Porcelain Penelope Show* had something to do with the myriad personas she had learned to rely on instead of becoming her own person. (She also knew the title.)

You might say, "Oh, Christ, we've seen that plot a million times." Well, we've seen most plots a million times. What makes a solo show work is finding the truth in it, and creating material that transports your audience. It has to start with the words, but there are other things you can add to the mix. That's where I come in.

During our first meeting, I almost always ask, "Do you have any special skills? Can you wiggle your nose or walk on water? Sing an Italian aria, maybe?" Precious can walk on stilts, juggle, tap dance, and sing badly on purpose, so there were limitless theatrical possibilities to bring her material to life. It is also my responsibility to read between the lines for subtext that may be too painful for the writer to initially acknowledge. However, I must not venture too abruptly into terrain that might be too sensitive for my student's psyche. I knew that Precious' father was Tommy Chong, of Cheech and Chong, and I could hear veiled (and not-so-veiled) references to him in the material she initially brought in. I assumed that part of her role playing as a survival tactic was the direct result of her tumultuous Hollywood life as the daughter of a very famous man.

PENELOPE

My papa? He's so big, people fall over when they see him so watch out. He's so bright, he's like an eclipse so you better wear your sunglasses or you might damage your retina. To some, he's like Jesus or Elvis but to me? Well, he's just my dad.

So, have we seen this plot a million times before? Not really, although the fear of being self-indulgent is a good check for any solo writer or performer. The dance of fiction versus nonfiction, biography versus autobiography, and all the potential blurring of those lines that is permissible would inform Precious' show as we took it through its many incarnations.

The story line—or plot, if you will—can distort, twist, and come in and out of focus, but there must be a core truth that emanates from the heart. Or guts. Or soul. Maybe all three. Otherwise, put on a show for your relatives at the next family reunion but don't hit the boards.

It is not my job to impose my story line or make my statement. It is my job to guide the performer-writer and push them into areas that are confrontational, embarrassing, and often painful. As a director, it is also my job to make the work theatrical, working with the particular abilities of the artist. When working on Syd Rushing's *Brothers Tellin'*, I remembered that this talented man can tap dance, a fact that I filed away in my head and relied on when one of his monologues—despite stunning writing—simply wasn't coming alive. It was the story of a typical black man enduring the day-to-day humiliations of being other than white, including getting pulled over by the cops for no real reason.

"Try tap dancing while you say those words," I suggested. "Spit them out as your body expresses the character's pent-up rage." It worked like magic. We eventually brought in a choreographer to fine-tune the idea.

EVAN

Yes, yes, officer, my ID is in the left-hand pocket. Yes, the car. It belongs to me and my girlfriend. Naw, it's just a hooptie. Uh, uhm. I work. Five days a week, fifty hours plus for the Post Office. No food stamps here. No, we don't live in this neighborhood, we were just passing through, going out to our favorite club. Yeah, I dance. Uh . . . uhm, thanks, thanks, thanks, officer . . . My name is Evan and I'm a black man. At least today I am. Yes, I prefer to be called black even though

I've been told I'm African American. Hey, listen to this, this white guy comes over from South Africa to the states, but his information says he's African American. Makes sense, he's from Africa and now he's American. So he insists on keeping that title even though black people tell him he oughta change it. What difference does it make though? I mean, in 300 years, we've gone from African! (Beko! Beko! Beko!) to Negro (ro, row, Ne-gro ro, row) to colored. Lawd knows the trouble I've seen. Lawd knows the trouble with black! Get aboard the free- dom train, we're bogeying into the seventies where black was wonderful, beautiful, wonderful! To Hallelujah! Hallelujah! African American! Somebody give me a Tums. Yeah, that's what I want to know: what is the "N word"? I see these reporters on TV talking about so and so said the "N word" to so and so. So what is the N word? Never? Novocain? Nerve? Nuisance? Nemesis? So, I guess we're Nubians in this millennium. Maybe, Ebonettes? But help me out here, 'cause I'm figurin' do I need anyone to tell me what box to fit in? . . . 'Cause I know I'm on *Candid Camera, Cops Caught in the Act, World's Dumbest Niggers!* Mr. DeMille, I'm ready for my African American closeup. You see, I know the cameras are rolling when I walk into a Macy's or a 7-11 and the store clerk says to me in the key of hate, "May I help you?" Which means "Does your black ass have money or are you planning to steal?" African American doesn't stop that woman from holding her purse a little tighter. African American doesn't stop that door from shutting, shutting, shutting in your face and leaving you with a Michael Jackson nose. And it never, ever, never made you, me, or anybody else more American. And it didn't stop *Homeboys from Outer Space* from coming on television. When I saw that mess on TV, I thought it was time to start picking cotton. Things are better though. I was pulled over fourteen times in '98! And in '99, whew, only eleven! Where's Johnny Cochran when you need him? Yeah, what if we all had a Johnny Cochran angel? Bell curves, hell curves, Jim Crow whadda' know? Those cops rather see me in a cell than a college. But that's okay 'cause you see my girlfriend, partner, significant other, equal, better half is

American, by way of the Irish. So now she drives at night, dark, at sundown . . . So we don't get detained, apprehended, pulled over. Hey, it works! Hey, you gotta do the dance or you end up in a box.

Would I suggest that Eugene Paulish, the writer with little experience on the boards, do a tap dance? No way. That would have been artificial and forced. In his autobiographical story about lost love, Eugene relies on the fantasy that Stevie Nicks would understand his heartache even if no one else did.

I was able to get him, in spite of his lack of stage experience, to gracefully and convincingly move around a couple of chairs that believably created a bistro, a train compartment, and a double bed. It gave *But Stevie Nicks Understands* a visual component that distinguished it from being the equivalent of a literary reading.

If time allows during the first meeting, I also ask, How do you see your show? Literally. What does it look like? What are the visual components? Is the look realistic or impressionistic? Is there a chair or a stool? Slide projections? Do you plan to change costumes? Will you have props (real or imagined)? A lighting concept? Follow spot or flashlights?

Again, this is not a test, but in many cases the look of the show will determine some writing choices. Or perhaps the writing choices will determine the look of the show. In either case, it demands consideration at the beginning of the process and allows the look to change—drastically, if necessary—as the piece evolves. My advice is to always go with what is simplest and forces the audience to engage their imagination more than they would if they were going to see a realistic production of *A Long Day's Journey into Night*.

Expense must also be a consideration. Most initial leaps into solo are self-produced. So you might consider keeping your day job and letting go of the revolving stage that moves from a haunted mansion to a sandy beachfront. Seriously, you should design your show so that it is affordable and practical. Keep costumes, props, and set pieces to a minimum. You'll thank me if you find yourself on tour, when carrying a hatbox can seem daunting. In *intimacies* and *more intimacies*, I created a dozen characters by manipulating a long red scarf into, among other things, a wig, a sling, a belt, a religious vestment, and an eye patch.

Precious is a gal who comes with costumes galore. And shoes! She also has a quirky but strong visual sense and a feel for color and texture. From the way she described the characters, often in terms of what they would wear or an activity that they might perform, I knew her show would scream for vibrant wardrobe with complementary props. Within reason, of course.

Precious collects and saves costumes and costume pieces. This is not the case for most performers so I strongly suggest that you simplify costuming along with other technical aspects of your show. Many performers choose to wear something neutral so that the color comes from the words, not the fabrics.

Could *The Porcelain Penelope Show* have been done with fewer costumes? Perhaps, but because the characters are show people who are poised to go on stage, we were grateful that Precious had closets of stuff to pull from and we didn't go broke buying glam outfits. Inherently theatrical, her characters were often defined by what they wore (or didn't wear).

In terms of lighting, which is limited in most solo venues for a variety of reasons, the look would be as theatrical as we could get it—showbizzy, razzle-dazzle, knock 'em dead.

You should see as many solo shows as possible: to inspire you and help you avoid some of the obvious pitfalls. "Educate yourself," Mark Travis advises. "Learn not only from what you see them do on stage, learn also from your experience as an audience member. Be aware of how they touched you, reached you, excited you, bored you, frustrated you, confused you.

"And remember, this is not about them. This experience is about you. You are learning about who you are as you are watching their show. And it is your reaction, your personal emotional journey, that is the gift received."

From a very practical standpoint, keep programs or write yourself notes about potential directors and designers. Solo show? Yeah, right. If you don't know anything about lighting or costumes or props, hire someone—someone you trust—who does.

Raymond Thompson has been lighting my solo work for more than fifteen years and I have a hard time imagining working without his contribution. He totally understands what I'm trying to do in my material and is able to light it accordingly.

Trusting your partners—whether the director or the proprietor of the space where you're working—will give you a sense of safety that will determine your level of freedom as an artist. We all make mistakes, but you do not want to develop an atmosphere of distrust that zaps all your creative energy.

Establishing trust doesn't always happen during the first encounter, but everything with Precious would prove to be accelerated. As our session was concluding, I felt we were beginning to trust each other. As a team, however, we would also need to trust the material—every word and every movement—before daring to present it to an audience.

Trust allows team players to create fully, opening the emotional, physical, and vocal conduits that will reveal the story and themes. Without trust, creative energy is blocked and the possibility for a viable piece is doomed.

Exercise/Trust

Find a quiet place with minimal distractions. If you are comfortable writing on a computer, fine. But if you like to do your first draft with pen and paper (I'm addicted to those yellow legal pads), that's fine, too. Simply think of an incident that happened to you around the time that you went to kindergarten—something that defines who you are today.

Please do not spend a lot of time in your head. Trust that your memories are stronger than you might think and that there may be more to the story than you immediately recognize. Just choose the event and write about it.

Spend no less than fifteen minutes and no more than half an hour. Do not worry about spelling or punctuation or sentence structure or anything technical. Just go for it. Be descriptive. Try to remember something spoken. The weather. Colors. And if don't remember details, it's okay to make them up. This isn't a test. Trust your words.

Chapter 1 Checklist

- Can you put your ego on hold and trust a teacher or director?
- Do you trust your abilities as a writer?
- Do you trust your abilities as a performer?
- Do you trust your voice?
- Do you trust your body?
- Do you trust your life experiences?
- Do you trust your imagination?
- Do you trust your ability to capture an audience?
- Can you trust an audience?
- Do you trust that you have something to say?
- What does your show look like (physically)? Furniture? Lighting? Special effects from hell? Do you trust your vision?
- Have you begun to make a list of directors and designers—ideally, trustworthy ones—whom you might call upon?
- Unless you have a backer, do you trust that you can raise, beg, borrow, or steal enough money to put on a solo show?

2 Energy

It takes enormous energy to drive a solo performance. Remember that you are the engine of the evening. Your energy determines exactly where the evening is headed.

Alec Mapa

Precious possesses energy. While "energy" has many meanings, I am referring to the intangible communication that sparks human connections; whether she's walking into a grocery store or vamping onstage as a wanton stripper, her energy pulls you in. And doesn't let go.

Don't confuse this with narcissistic preening. The energy I'm describing is accessible, vulnerable, and free. This particular quality is not the hallmark of all actors, which is precisely why not all actors—even accomplished ones—have the stuff that's necessary to engage an audience for an hour plus, alone, on a stage.

"I think most performers are not aware of the enormous challenge of performing solo," Mark Travis says, "and of the enormous opportunities.

"Performing solo should be designated as a singular performing art. It is not traditional acting (many highly trained and highly skilled actors struggle valiantly with solo performing). It is not stand-up. It's intended to look easy, relaxed, personal, and improvisational. It requires learning new skills and abandoning certain 'rules' of acting.

"Most performers new to the solo process view this art form as traditional theatre. It is not. In traditional theatre we watch a story unfold. In solo performing we are taken on a ride by a storyteller, the story unfolds, not in front of us but within our own individual imaginations. It is closer to the novel or radio than it is to traditional theatre and film."

In *Getting Your Solo Act Together*, Rob Sullivan said, "I don't know if [energy] can be taught. It takes a certain ability to fill the space with energy and draw people in. Not a lot of people have this ability." This is not a needy energy; rather it is a force that comforts, invites, shares, and empowers.

Brian Clark has remained one of my best friends for more than thirty years. During those decades, Brian achieved a substantial track record as a live musician in St. Louis. His endurance is based on the necessary combination of talent and sheer energy. Over the years, I've repeatedly seen him perform and inevitably compared his evolution as an artist to mine. A singer, far more than an actor, is often cast in the role of seducer. And Brian was always deliciously seductive.

Like me and many performers, one of his initial motives for giving so much onstage was to find some degree of self-acceptance. But self-acceptance in the glare of the spotlight is only one short step away from self-delusion (not to mention self-indulgence), and before you know it the desire to be loved overshadows the performance and the performer's responsibility to be present and share, and weakens the show's effect.

When I recently saw Brian perform, there had been a palpable shift. No longer was he using the audience to bolster his self-esteem. As a result, his stage persona emanated a newfound purity that had not existed earlier, and that made him more exciting and created a more engaging experience for his audience. The desire to be loved can drive a performance (and a career) only so far. Brian attributes his evolution to putting the audience before himself. Of course!

In straight plays, the fourth wall, that line of demarcation between actor and audience, can provide the actor with a safety zone. With very few exceptions, however, it is incumbent upon the soloist to tear down the fourth wall so that a synergy exists between performer and audience member. Even if the performer is not working autobiographically or is playing a not particularly likable character, there must be an exchange that is more intimate and intense than what most actors experience. The connection between the performer (storyteller) and the audience must become the most vital part of the entire event. The performer actually creates a relationship with a new audience each night that is vital, complex, and compelling. This is very challenging. Many actors, as we know, feel comfort in hiding—in the character, in the fictional writing, and in the event. In solo performing, there is no place to hide. And if it is autobiographical, you are bound to feel naked.

Rob Sullivan finds a comfort level doing solo that he has never managed to find when performing the work of other writers. "If I didn't write the words, it sounds phony when it comes out of my mouth." He's being a bit hard on himself, but the organic aspect of performing your own work is pure, often allowing you to go places on stage where you've never gone before.

"The hard part is letting the audience be who they are," Alec Mapa says. One of the current darlings of solo work, Mapa has created several heartfelt pieces, written and performed seamlessly. "If they're unresponsive, *let* them be. Pushing will only result in yelling. Louder isn't always better, and sometimes that'll just alienate folks further. Again, respect the audience. Honor the fact that they've shown up and just tell the story. Sometimes rapt fascination can be expressed in complete silence."

There are no lessons in how to achieve this level of energy. As Mama Rose says in her one-woman show within a show ("Rose's Turn" from *Gypsy*), "Some people got it and make it pay, some people can't even give it away." That is why there are some solo performers (many of whom refer to themselves as "performance artists") who can't spell "Stanislavski" or tell you the difference between a beat and an intention. But, if they have the requisite energy to connect with an audience, it doesn't matter. Tim Miller does not consider himself an actor, yet he has effortlessly been establishing a rapport with audiences all over the world for two decades. This is a talent that not all trained actors can possess. "I perform a lot," Miller says. "I put the finishing touches on a show in the audiences and the communities I encounter. Only after I've done a show quite a few times in different performance situations do I start to trust the material."

Having the requisite energy to capture an audience is only a starting point, however. The first destination, in my opinion, should always be at least one workshop performance that is not open to the general public or the press. Allow me to illustrate my point by sharing a Winona Ryder story.

The initial meeting that Precious and I had in the spring of 2002 coincided with my working on a project that was exciting, infuriating, and—in spite of the fact that it was flawed—had garnered more publicity than anything I had ever done. *My Name Is Winona and I'm a Shoplifter* was one of those ideas that someone was going to glom onto and I thought, why not me? For about five seconds, I considered playing the troubled movie star (I'd done Marilyn) but I just didn't have the energy to write, direct, produce, and act in *Winona,* which had to get on the boards sooner rather than later, while simultaneously working with Precious to meet an August deadline for our first workshop production.

Allowing myself to do something that I thought was uncharacteristically fluffy, the piece intentionally began as the equivalent of a *Saturday Night Live* sketch. Winona shows up at a twelve-step meeting for shoplifters and admits she has a problem in the midst of self-obsessive cell phone calls, recitations of her reviews in *Mr. Deeds,* and deliberately corny Top-Ten lists inspired by David Letterman.

In researching the young actress, there were many riveting details that as a writer I couldn't ignore. Her obsession with *Catcher in the Rye,* for one. Her relationship with godfather Timothy Leary for another. Then there was Winona's heartfelt experience of filming *Little Women* while involving herself with the Polly Klass case. (In 1993, the ten-year-old Polly was kidnapped from her bedroom at knifepoint and murdered. A search ensued and eventually her killer was given the death penalty.) So much for fluff.

As I had previously done with Marilyn, I took factual material and interwove it with speculation and imagination. When people asked me if Winona "really said that," there were times when truth and fiction had blurred and I couldn't actually remember. The same was true for my take on Marilyn.

I always envisioned Winona being played by a man and had to repeatedly explain why (to the press, among other folks). There are some things that are purely instinctive, but when members of the press enter the picture, you have to come up with some fairly intelligent responses. Aside from the camp element, I felt that unless you were going to have an actress do a spot-on imitation any attempt at verisimilitude would curtail artistic license. The entire process would be devoted to the reality of her impersonation and I didn't think that was very interesting. That said, I wanted an emotional energy to match the performer and the actress. Rex Lee had been studying with me for years, making real progress that had resulted in a considerable track record of television and film work.

One of the challenges in casting Winona was to find an actor who was a quick study; not only did the piece have to get on its feet immediately if not sooner, but there would also be constant rewrites. Rex has a vulnerable presence on stage that I thought was very appropriate for Winona, and he is highly intelligent—a quality possessed by the movie star as well as a quality needed to pull this project off. I wanted funny but I didn't want an actor to make fun of her; rather, I felt it necessary that the actor love her.

I take full responsibility for a project that was rushed to the stage in the name of commercial considerations. Rex was simply not ready. He told me he was not ready and I, in some state of denial, didn't really believe him.

On the day of the first performance, after the final dress rehearsal (which was a disaster but they always are), he tried to make me listen. I honestly thought it was simply a case of predictable nervousness. He'd worked his ass off, memorizing new pages on a daily basis as well as dealing with difficult costuming and hair and makeup.

With the press in attendance, the first performance was a mess. There were no previews; as sole financial producer, I couldn't afford them. We simply had to get it on its feet. We did one performance a week for four weeks and Rex, traumatized after the opening night debacle, made great leaps but always seemed slightly underrehearsed. I felt empathy but I was also pissed off—mostly at myself.

The *Los Angeles Times* was extremely kind—encouraging even. That started a media blitz that was international. I was interviewed on a radio show in Australia; an article appeared in the *TV Guide*; a photo in *W;* local newspapers did photo shoots, celebrities talked about it on morning talk shows. But guess what? It didn't live up to the hype.

After four performances, once a week, at the Zephyr in West Hollywood, we did several weekends at Studio A, a venue in another part of town. Rex began to nail it, but it was too late because the word of mouth was not as strong as it needed to be to make the show a success.

Immediately after the Los Angeles run, we got a booking in San Diego—two performances back-to-back in one night—and Rex was amazing. He finally had the energy that was demanded to make the show work. I had not been wrong about his ability, but I had dreadfully miscalculated the time needed to pull the show together. Even with my experience as a performer, I'm not sure I could have pulled it off. Consider the tasks: A man playing a woman, navigating daily rewrites during a two-week rehearsal period prior to an opening night with the press salivating.

By the time we got to San Diego, the pressure was off and Rex felt free. It was also an utterly different audience. Most of the Los Angeles audiences were predominately gay, but the San Diego theatre audiences were fairly run-of-the-mill and decidedly more straight than gay.

That's where I was forced to study the entire conceit of the show. In many ways, it was not hip enough for the queens in LA who probably had already done their own Winona impersonations, but it was just shocking, offensive, and titillating enough to capture a straight crowd two hours away on the freeway. While an evening in the theatre should not discriminate, it is unrealistic to think that all shows (especially solo shows, which tend to have an edge) are suitable for all markets.

What is your potential audience? If you're writing a show that only your high school graduation class will understand, I'd rethink it. On the other hand, if you think your story would play as well in San Francisco as it would in Des Moines, your theme may run the risk of being too general. I'm not suggesting that you limit yourself by writing to a target audience nor am I saying that your piece should avoid finding a universal theme. What I am saying is to consider the demographics and realize there are discrepancies in audiences' level of tolerance, vocabulary, and understanding.

I once did an evening of solo (a compilation of various pieces, which included playing women) for an Alcoholics Anonymous convention in LA. The audience, largely comprised of recovering lesbians, loathed my work. (Note that I avoided saying they hated me, although I think some of them did.)

The very next night, I performed the exact same show—word for word—at a conference for men in Tucson, Arizona, and received a spontaneous standing ovation.

I can only guess why the lesbians reacted so negatively. In some lesbian circles (and the vigilant recovery community might be one of them), a man playing a woman is offensive, period, as are specific depictions of male sexuality. At the top of the show, I performed Big Red, a black female street hooker, followed by an erotically charged excerpt from James Carroll Pickett's *Dream Man*.

I've grown weary of that "preaching to the choir" analogy, which suggests that in some instances, an audience is on your side before they find their seat and, as a result, the experience isn't valid. I really don't believe that so-called choir exists. People, no matter how many similarities they share, are more complex than that. Ask any choir member if there aren't Republicans and Democrats, rich and poor, young and old, well educated and not, singing in the choir.

I always like a few choirboys in my audience (those who are decidedly on my side) but, more important, I want audience members who challenge me. When I walk on stage, a significant part of my job is to take everyone in that audience on a ride they have never been on before. Fasten your seatbelts and all that jazz. That said, I count many lesbians among my greatest supporters and I know many men are completely turned off by what I do. Bottom line? Don't stereotype or underestimate your potential audience. But know that a joke might land differently in Capetown than it does in Provincetown.

The process with Precious could not have been more different. I was probably wearing too many hats on the *Winona* project. With *The*

Porcelain Penelope Show, my primary focus was conducting the train as it moved from one station to the next.

Our first station stop was setting the date for the workshop performance, a critical decision because it imposes a deadline on the first phase of the process which, without a specific game plan, could go on for years. The workshop also provides the artist and the director with the opportunity to be certain that the relationship is working.

I do not commit to being the show's official director nor do I have any stake in the show's future until after the workshop takes place. The financial situation remains an hourly rate, which is applied to my fee if we mutually agree to move toward a full production as a team.

"A couple of months," Precious said when I asked her how soon she envisioned putting something on its feet to show to a limited audience. Her ambition was astounding, but as we began meeting—sometimes once a week, sometimes twice—I knew that she'd have a show that was at least presentable in a couple of months.

We began working on the text in my living room/office rather than spending money to rent a rehearsal space. We fleshed out the characters, tried to place them in the most effective order, and strengthened how they were related (or not) so that there was a reason they were appearing on the same bill. The energy necessary to revise material is obvious and this is where many aspiring soloists prove lazy.

As an example, Sue (not her real name) came to me with pages and pages of what she had come up with in a writing class. She read me several of the pieces and I agreed that she had a substantial story to tell but that it needed to be drastically reworked if the essays were going to be transformed into a theatre piece. Oh, and she was a singer and insisted on performing a lot of Barbra Streisand songs.

I gently suggested that we hold off on the singing aspect of the piece until we achieved some coherent structure with the written material, knowing that I would nix the Streisand numbers. I'm not saying that I wouldn't be open to her singing, but I'd strongly suggest original material in lieu of relying on standards to help tell her story. I am reluctant to use any familiar music in a solo show that is chosen in order—too often cheaply, in my opinion—to elicit an emotional response.

At our second meeting, she brought the same notebook and read a few more of the essays, but had not written a new sentence and virtually ignored all of my suggestions as she brainstormed out loud about her ideas. I'm not saying that my ideas were better than hers, but if you don't bring in something that is alive and jumps off the page, I'm gonna get real bored. She also brought a CD to remind me of her skills as a vocalist. We were going nowhere fast.

I think she cancelled a session or two, and at our third session she admitted that she really didn't feel she was "ready" to do a solo show. I agreed. She simply didn't have the emotional energy that is required to go from talking about doing a solo show to actually writing a solo show.

"How much time do you have and how much are you willing to dedicate to this process?" is a question Mark Travis suggests you ask yourself. "Your choice of doing a solo show is no different than wanting to become an Olympic athlete," he says. "Same dedication. Same training schedule. Same roller-coaster ride of victories and failures. Same risks. Same potential victories at the end. It's a long, hard road. Be willing to make the sacrifice, take your time, seek all the best coaches and managers you can, and remember—you are the only one who can drive it to completion."

I often hear myself saying, "This may not be exactly right, but maybe it will give you a direction to move in." I'll suggest a different word, punch up a joke, beg you to make cuts and help you find the right note, but I will not write your show. Because I'm a writer, I think some people assume I'll do the writing for them. Precious wrote like a wild woman, taking some of my suggestions and rejecting others but always delivering fresh material with a new spin.

In many instances, it's simply a matter of energizing the material. What plays on the page doesn't necessarily play on the stage. In many instances, the character (and this includes the autobiographical self-written "character") is written passively and lacks color: "And then I got in the car with my dad, who drove us to the lake" is a sentence that requires energizing.

First of all, make it immediate. "I'm in the car with my dad and he's driving us to the lake." That's better but I still want more. What kind of car? What color? What kind of day is it? Sunny? Cloudy? Raining? How far away is the lake? Is there a radio in the car? What's playing? Here's where I also stress the axiom "Don't let the truth get in the way of a good story." If rain deepens the emotionality of the story you are telling, have it rain. Or perhaps rain is the perfect contrast to the picture you're trying to paint. Even though the radio was off, you could have Elvis singing in the background if it somehow illuminates your story. The car is white? If red creates the mood you're after, make it red.

You might end up with something like this: "I am in the car with my dad, who loves listening to a station that plays old Elvis songs. It starts to rain while the King sings, 'Are You Lonesome Tonight?' and I am grateful that the downpour will wash away the embarrassing dirt on his ancient white Rambler. With no indication that the rain will let up, I wonder why we continue heading to the lake for a fishing trip. Maybe the sound of Elvis' voice is drowning out the sound of the rain."

Another consideration is to avoid writing what you can act. Show us, don't tell us. If the line reads, "Then the bastard told me to get out and I felt like I was going to have a breakdown," you don't need to say, "and I felt like I was going to have a breakdown." Act that phrase. Also avoid descriptive adjectives or adverbs when quoting someone (especially yourself). "'I'm so sorry,' I said, facetiously" doesn't require "facetiously." Act it!

Precious caught on to this energizing process very quickly and it became apparent that it was time, after four or five meetings devoted to the text, to put the characters on their feet. I stress to my students that they don't have to have a perfect script, that in fact getting the piece on its feet might well show them where changes need to be made in the text. In other words, don't think a perfect script is required before you take that big leap into the rehearsal studio.

Since Precious told me she had various skills when we first met, I asked her to bring in her bag of tricks—everything from juggling balls to those skinny balloons that can magically be transformed into animal shapes. We began matching an activity with a character, always finding ways to energize and deepen the emotional life of the storytelling. Don't insist on showing off your sword-swallowing skills, no matter how impressive, just because you can. The theatrics must serve the text.

Any physical activity must connect emotionally to the words. Don't impose movement if it's unnecessary. Don't impose movement for the sake of moving. And please don't wander around the stage aimlessly without motivation—a common mistake made by beginning solo performers. There is a fundamental fear of standing along on a stage, still.

The Sexy Mom, for example, is desperately trying to maintain her equilibrium in a world that has gone haywire. The choice for her to juggle was the perfect physical activity to mirror her inner struggle.

SEXY MOM

Sorry I'm late. Ernesto was teaching me a new turn in salsa class. I'm a sexy mom. Penelope's mother. But people say we look more like sisters. Because, well, I look young. I'm not going to tell you my age. But when we travel with Penelope's father, well, let's just say they think I'm his kid. The old man. Ha! Penelope needs to use her sexuality more. She needs to find herself a man. A rich man. One who'll buy her jewels, jewels, jewels. My mother—she did not marry well. Not that I believe in marriage because I don't. Too straight, too normal. But when I was a kid, we were poor. Eight kids. A dad who was a drunk. East Vancouver. I knew I needed out, out, out. It's about survival. That's what Penelope just doesn't understand. She needs to learn that you've got to tell men what to do. Why isn't she more like Gwyneth Paltrow? Honey, how do you get on the Internet thing? I want to write a check . . . It's a circus. I run this show.

"If you drop the balls, play it," I'd say. "That's precisely the metaphor of her conflict—she's determined not to drop the ball." As the Sexy Mom evolved, the juggling became even more organic to what she was saying and how she said it. What was also significant about this character and the Grandma character was that these pieces had more obviously autobiographical elements. While some of her other characters were certainly reflections of Precious, the details had been blurred beyond recognition. It was often easier to perform the Stripper Who Talks or the Snake Girl than to confront the confessional aspects of Sexy Mom and Grandma.

GRANDMA

Penelope hoodwinked me into appearing in her show but I'm not much of a performer. That's more my mother or my sister, Thelma. She liked to entertain. She entertained the boys that came over to visit us girls. She liked to entertain. I would play the piano and my mother would sing. "They say it's only a paper moon, hanging over . . . mmm . . . but it wouldn't be make-believe if you believed in me." My mother married a Ross. They were a very prominent family from Scotland. She almost married well. But he was disowned when he married her. She was a bastard child. For tonight's performance I'm going to make a tiny origami box. That's Oriental—origami. Those Orientals are so clean, they make everything so small and neat as a pin and they're all smart as whips. Now I like to use old cards. Penelope's mother got me the sweetest card. It had hummingbirds on it . . . Christmas cards, any sort of card will do because of the weight of the paper and it has a nice design on it already. Now you cut it like that. Now I like to make them small so I can fit, oh, I don't know, a little doll inside. Something tiny. It's a little surprise. I tried to teach them this over at the Senior Center at my crafts class. But they never get it right. Those girls. How old am I? None of your business. That's for me to know and for you never to find out. I'm sweet sixteen and never been kissed. I don't want to talk about the past. Everyone wants to know about the past. Snooping around. Nosey. There, now that's the box. Put it away. Put it away for later. I tell my kids, "Waste not, want not." Mary Dealy. My friend. She worked at that paper factory and earned enough to buy herself a condo with a view of the water. She smoked and drank and would lie out in the sun.

No, I never did. I wore hats and long-sleeved shirts and sat in the shade with my fair skin. Oh, my girls would laugh at me but look what they say now about the sun and skin cancer. I told my girls to save their skin.

The Snake Girl was the newest character, reflecting more timely stories that the writer-performer was expressing and observing. The creation of a character often relies on the combination of experience and observation. Even though it can be based on experience, the result is not entirely autobiographical because it is colored by observation or imagination.

Let's say something really profound happens to you—the death of a loved one, for example. If you aren't completely comfortable with detailing your response based entirely on factual information, let the power of observation and imagination join the process. You might remember a story someone told you about a similar situation. Or you may have observed someone who lost a loved one and remember their response. Or you might simply imagine other possible responses that heighten yours or make your experience more vivid.

The other way to go is to observe someone that you think would be an interesting character to create. In this case, you may weave some of your experience into what you've observed. And imagination can always play a part in strengthening or giving the character more life.

SNAKE GIRL

I was at this powwow. Yes, a powwow. And after the powwow, back at the Quality Inn, this woman—like a ghost—swooshes up to me. Scary, right? She looked like an X ray. An ancestral X ray. Powwow, snakes. Does that mean I'm a snake charmer? A snake tamer? A snake dancer? I mean, Adam and Eve and the snake, right? The original sin. It's biblical, right? I'm biblical. How can I be biblical? I grew up in Los Angeles. LA is not a biblical place. Maybe if you're Mexican. But me? I'm just some wannabe entertainer, over the hill, downward slope. I had an epiphany. After the powwow. In my motel room at the Quality

Inn. Q is for Quality. I'm watching cable but I smell cucumbers everywhere. I want to work at a snake store here in Cherokee, Snakes Alive. The sign is neon script green. Deadly snakes, king snakes, cobras, green ones, tiny red ones. I'm going to wrangle them up. A snake dancer, a snake charmer. I'm afraid of being devoured. That old woman. Am I old? Am I the crazy X ray lady? I want to start over. Drew did it. I can, too. Can I look up to someone who is younger than me? Everyone is younger than me. Everyone has always been younger than me. I'm the snake lady, the reptile girl. If you can't beat 'em, join 'em. I want to die. Help me, help me, please. Snake lady. Snake girl. I'm the snake girl. I see it. One bit my nipple. Ouch. Cleopatra. The asp, asp, asp. A slithery, sleek bloodless snakeskin. Ssssssssssssssssssssssssssssssssssssssssssssssssssssssssssssssssssssssssssss ssssssssssssssssssssssssssssssssssss.

Precious had already conceived Porcelain Penelope's song and hyperkinetic tap dance, complete with a music tape.

PORCELAIN

Porcelain Penelope I'm so cute
People wanna see me in my birthday suit
"P" is for Porcelain
"P" is for Penelope
"P" is for pretty terrific I'd say

As other characters began to blossom, several things fell into place. Even though the theme was amorphous at this early stage, it was clear that these characters were somehow related (sometimes literally) to Precious. They were aspects of her fractured self that she summoned at various times in order to survive. Having them appear in a nightclub setting seemed like the perfect theatrical device.

At some point, we decided to put the backstage/dressing room area upstage of the playing area so that there was a line of demarcation between her "real" self and the various selves who leaped on the stage to perform.

There was also Mr. H, the theatre owner and emcee of the show, who called the shots. "The dictator of my psyche" is how Precious described him.

Mr. H

Save your boring anecdotes for your Lifetime Television Intimate Portrait. If they ever call you back. Oh, well, on with the show. I am delighted to introduce our next performer . . .

What he represented was her inner critic who continually made fun of her and threatened to fire her. This was based on the male voices in her life who played the role of insensitive critic and who could be perceived as having power over her career.

And we cannot forget Penelope's nemesis, her Talking Vagina, who got hairier as the show unraveled.

Talking Vagina

I'm allowed to have an opinion. This is a free country. Ever hear of the first amendment? This Bush has rights, too!

Penelope

I'm going to level with you guys. Stuff is happening. Down there. And it's really freaking me out. My vagina. It's pretty hairy and scary and I keep trimming it. But pretty soon I won't be able to do this little girl act anymore. I hate it. I want to be smooth and pink . . . Barbie, I am not . . . My vagina sings songs. It likes to sing and I can't stop it.

The Vagina's voice was somewhere between Harvey Fierstein's and Mercedes MacCambridge's. Three pairs of underpants, with various lengths of hair sewn on them, were preset on the set. During certain costume changes, she'd switch from one pair to another hairier pair so the audience would see that the Talking Vagina was indeed growing uncontrollably.

While the characters were taking on lives of their own, Precious was also securing an appropriate space for the August performances. Although she was adamant about the workshop performances of her show being done in a theatre space, it is not necessary in all cases. Because of the inherent theatricality of *The Porcelain Penelope Show,* I understood her desire to put on a show—modestly produced, but a show with razzamataz nonetheless.

Precious had the energy and commitment to back up her aspirations but her ambition never crossed over into the grandiose. From the very beginning, she wanted the first incarnation of her show to be considerably more than a "staged reading" and she put in the hours that were required to make that happen.

However, if your piece is less physical or less complex in terms of production values, you could do "a workshop" in someone's home or in a very inexpensive rehearsal space. Or even in the local bookstore (if any of those exist anymore). I definitely suggest a less strenuous approach when working with someone with less stage experience. It's certainly acceptable to ease into a workshop situation.

Although I can't remember one single example of a student taking my advice, it really would be permissible, and even advisable, to carry a script during a workshop performance. For many reasons, most performers invest too much energy in learning lines (as if that gives the performance life) instead of rewriting. Trust me, eventually you will rewrite and you'll have to relearn as well. Please don't give that excuse about not being able to act with a script in your hand; I and countless others have done some of our best acting holding on to a script.

The primary goal of a workshop is to introduce a third energy to the process, those who bear witness, completing the triangular relationship between performer, director, and audience. What works? What doesn't? Are they getting it? Is it understandable? Are the laughs well placed? No matter how dense the language is or how complex the theme is, it must be clear enough for an audience to understand and have an emotional experience.

On those workshop nights, I often pay as much (or more) attention to the audience than I do the performer, checking to see if they are confused at any point or when they lose interest. That said, I strongly suggest that you not make drastic changes or adjustments based on one audience's response. It is simply a gauge. I am also particularly leery of listening to friends' or relatives' critiques. Please don't tell me, "My best friend said he didn't realize I had so much sex appeal" or "My mom loves it when I do that pouting thing." If nothing else, your friends and family members who say such things are reviewing you, not your work. It's important to have a support network, but uncritical support is no support at all.

As my work with Precious intensified, there was a meeting I had to honor regarding a solo show I'd worked on earlier in the year. This was a situation where the writer-performer put his friends' uncritical feedback before my critical feedback—and the result wasn't pretty. Clark (not his real name) had written a piece with six characters strung together with a flimsy but workable thread. The writing was truly inspired and grew increasingly rich during the weeks prior to the workshop performances.

The acting paled by comparison. With the exception of a couple of the pieces, the workshop performances showed that the actor was unequal to the material, even though he had written it. Because I was fond of Clark, this would not be easy to put into words. Part of me wanted to bullshit him and direct the piece as it was. But the part of me that respects the art of solo theatre (not to mention my own reputation) simply could not take this project to the next level in good conscience without a major overhaul.

I began the meeting by praising his writing and his stellar work habits. I reiterated that I felt his writing was extraordinary but I honestly felt he should consider splitting the roles between himself and two more actors, allowing him to play two of the characters and giving two of the more challenging characters to actors with more experience and training.

I said all of this as gently as I could but I could feel his resistance. He was hurt and angry and defensive. He was also blinded by the praise of his friends and began a litany of "my friends said this" and "my friends said that." He took my suggestions and my criticism as an attack, and there was nothing that would change that.

I don't want to work with doormats. I love to be proven wrong, it can be very exciting. But if you come to me as a student, if you want me to direct you, you're accepting that I can see the work more clearly than you can, that I know more about acting and solo performance than your friends. "It's important to have someone, whose opinion you respect," Alec Mapa says, "to bounce ideas off. I've benefited enormously from my collaboration with the playwright Chay Yew. He's a brilliant writer and director and shares the same short attention span I do. I respect his opinion, so if I've an idea that doesn't interest him, chances are it isn't stageworthy. This trust has come only after years of collaborating and it hasn't been without incident."

In any collaboration, confrontations happen. It's how both parties handle them that indicates whether the collaboration will flourish. Days before the first workshop performances, Precious and I experienced our first bit of friction. While I do not have a contract drawn up at the workshop stage, I pretty much assume my name will be attached to any promotional material.

Imagine my shock when I saw the postcard announcing the workshop production of *The Porcelain Penelope Show* with an adorable picture of Precious as a little girl, striking a pose in her glittery dance ensemble, on the front and all the pertinent info on the back. All the pertinent info, that is, with the exception of the director's name.

I tried to let it go, telling myself that she was simply overwhelmed with details and forgot. Yet another part of me felt that it was, on some level, intentional. Maybe she wanted to take all the credit. Did she resent what I'd brought to the table? Or was it merely a sincere mistake?

Within hours of my seeing it, there was a phone message and she apologized her guts out, saying that she'd already had a sticker made with my name on it and she was "really, really sorry."

But the following morning at rehearsal, she offered another explanation. She was sitting on the floor of the rehearsal studio when I arrived and in the midst of an extended apology with lots of tears, she said, "Maybe it's because I don't feel you are really as involved as I thought you'd be. Or you don't care as much."

A contract would have been useful, I thought to myself, trying to recover from her honest but, in my opinion, somewhat harsh observation. I knew that my hurt was secondary to hers, and I also knew that I had to be the adult here and not let myself be guilt-tripped. I'll admit that I was extremely busy going from project to project and often might have seemed distracted. We were also in what I considered to be the early stages of a process, which I think she perceived as being much further along. My dedication may have seemed less in comparison to hers, but that's not an unusual situation in a solo collaboration where the writer-performer is essentially also the producer.

"Precious," I said. "This is an unusual situation for you. You are accustomed to having a producer in charge of booking the theatre, hiring the technicians, and overseeing the publicity. You are not only the writer-performer," I explained. "You are your own producer. That may be why it seems like I'm less invested." She seemed to understand and I was confident that time would prove that my investment was considerable.

In retrospect, I also feel that this might have been the first example of her casting me in the role of the withholding or absent father. The unavailable dad theme was evident in the script. It was probably easy to impose it on me. Over the next two years, we would play various roles with each other and this dynamic would be one of them. And I'll admit that I was part of the equation—it takes two to tango. Or put on a solo show.

That said, we had a show to put on, honey, and we were both smart enough not to let this skirmish jeopardize the energy we needed for the imminent performances. In reality, it probably cemented the beginning of a dramatic collaboration.

According to Dan Kwong, "Collaboration is the art of disagreement." Based on his history of solo work, energized by the input of other artists, Kwong would know.

Exercise/Energy

Remember that passage you wrote? It's time to put it on its feet; it's time to give it energy. And do some editing. Find a place where you have enough room to comfortably move about (I'm not kidding when I tell you that I often rehearse in parks).

Spend at least half an hour and no more than an hour reading the material and making appropriate edits based on how it feels when it's spoken out loud. And equally important, notice how the words feel in your body as you walk. Or run. Or skip. Or maybe lie down.

Don't restrict your movement to being realistic. Or attempting to mime things. (Please don't pick up an imaginary knife and fork if you're at dinner.) In fact, contrast what you do physically with what you're saying. Give what you've written energy. Let the words land. Say them several different ways, in several different positions.

You'll inevitably change the order of things (or, might not). And you also might remember something juicy to add—that's fine, too. And when you bring your physical self into the piece, blue might become purple, or a rainy afternoon might turn into a hailstorm.

Remember to avoid quotes written in the past tense. Tell us, "I am a bit cranky today" as opposed to "I was a bit cranky that day." And whatever you do, don't act like a child (Lily Tomlin did Edith Ann, but she's one of very few adults who can play children).

Oh. Have fun.

Chapter 2 Checklist

- Do you have the energy needed to write and rewrite (and rewrite and rewrite)?

- Do you have the physical energy to do a solo performance?

- Do you have the vocal energy to do a solo performance?

- Do you have the energy to connect intimately with an audience?

- Are you rushing to meet an opening night deadline without doing a series of workshops and/or previews?
- Set a deadline for a workshop performance or a preview so you have a specific goal to reach.
- Define your potential audience but don't limit yourself.
- Do you have the time necessary to devote to a solo show?
- Do you know the difference between a support network and fawning family and friends?
- Do you understand that, as a solo artist, you will inevitably be part of the production team in addition to being the writer and performer?

3 Collaboration

Without free exchange of ideas between those who make art, how can they ever engage the humanity they purport to reflect and challenge? When performing, I inevitably learned more from my collaborators than my own explorations, often lasting well beyond the end of the project.

David Nichols

The tech rehearsal scheduled for the afternoon of the first workshop performance of *The Porcelain Penelope Show* was delayed because I had a nasty infection in my thumb, requiring a doctor's appointment. But Precious and I were in sync and her friend Amy O'Neill (a wonderful actress-artist) helped her pull things together, including building a door frame that would delineate the boundary between the backstage area and the onstage playing space. Amy was a collaborator of the first order.

They also hung a clothesline that extended across the entire length of the upstage area that held dozens of outlandish costumes, some of which were practical and others chosen simply to create a kaleidoscopic burst of color.

Precious had selected a hip Hollywood venue, the Elephant Theatre, for the initial two-night run in August of 2002. In addition to dozens of her friends, the opening-night audience of this workshop production included Precious' agent, her therapist, the artistic director of Highways (Danielle Brazell), and the couple who run the Zephyr Theatre (Gary Guidinger and Linda Toliver). And unless I'm dreaming this, Zelda Rubinstein was in the house.

As the house began to fill up, I made frequent visits to her dressing room to see how she was holding up. She had made that magical transformation from fatigued worker bee to radiant presence, poised to face her audience. It isn't merely hair and makeup that create the change; it's as if some inner switch turns from off to on.

I noticed a huge bouquet of white roses. "An admirer?" I teased.

"Yes," she said, and we shared a knowing we've-been-through-this-before laugh. At this moment, she was less concerned with her love life and more concerned with whether her parents had arrived. "Check once more," she said.

"Okay, honey," I said.

They had not arrived. Although the house was full and it was past eight, she insisted on waiting a bit longer. Because her entrance is ostensibly from the street and she had a lengthy hike from the dressing room to the street that led to the theatre entrance, we had to coordinate the start of the show with the stage manager.

Finally, she decided to start the show without them.

The following day, Precious shrugged it off by explaining that they had trouble with plane connections. It didn't seem to diminish her excitement about what we'd accomplished. Although the show was by no means perfect yet, there was no question that we were on to something. Even at this early stage, *The Porcelain Penelope Show* was funny, moving, and provocative.

I was at once most pleased and angered by Precious' agent's comment that she needed to "calm down." Translation from Hollywoodspeak: "You are too fucking much and you got on my nerves." Great, I thought to myself. We got him going. On the other hand, I have dealt with Hollywood squeamishness for too many years now and it pissed me off. Precious knew that this project was not likely going to enhance a mainstream television and film career. Still, it was disconcerting to hear his response. In a matter of weeks she sought new representation, determined to find someone who understood and valued the range of her talents.

Seated next to her agent that night was her therapist, who had strongly encouraged her to do the show "as a ritual" in order to further explore the various aspects of her personality and the dynamics of her family. I would caution anyone against using the stage as a psychiatrist's couch. On the other hand, how can a piece that is ripped from one's inner life not be a therapeutic experience? No one was more concerned than Precious that the show not come off as a therapy session.

We've all seen the solo show that is loaded with self-indulgent psychobabble where the performer appears to be competing for the Best Victim Award. Whatever catharsis a performer might experience as a result of doing a solo show must not happen in front of an audience. You are there to provide *them* with a catharsis. Save your own catharsis for the rehearsal hall, your dressing room, or your car on the way home from the show.

We made a few minor adjustments after the first performance. Although it lacked the exuberance of the workshop's opening, her second performance showed us where to infuse *The Porcelain Penelope Show* with even more depth and truth, excitement, and razzle-dazzle, meaning and purpose. We needed to analyze, edit, rewrite, finesse, discuss, strengthen, and gain confidence. We didn't need to "calm down."

First and foremost, we would look at the acting and writing choices with a microscope—page by page, moment by moment—always attempting to make them clearer, crisper, and cleaner.

The really terrific news was that Gary Guidinger and Linda Toliver at the Zephyr were willing to cut a good deal for us to ease into a run at their theatre.

Founded in 1956, the Zephyr is on the brink of its fiftieth birthday celebration, having established itself as one of Los Angeles' most consistent and respected theatre spaces.

My history with the Zephyr goes back more than twenty years. In 1980, I coproduced a series of Sunday matinee performances of Rob Sullivan's luminous *Flower Ladies and Pistol Kids*. Also in the eighties, I redirected Emmett Foster's *A One-Mormon Show*, when Harry Hart-Browne replaced writer-performer Foster.

ROB

Bad thoughts. Bad thoughts and trouble. But once upon a time, I was in love. Used to get a phone call late at night. "Hello, will you come over and see me? It's only thirty miles away and I miss you." "I miss you, too." "Then get on the bus and get on over here." "Okay, I will." Then I'd get on the bus and I'd see people alone and people in pairs and all the while I'd feel her getting closer to me. And I'd look out the bus window and see the lights of the city and the darkness of the ocean. Then I'd get to her town. Walk up her hill. Tall pine trees, the fog falling over the mountain and everything looking real ancient. At the top of her hill I'd come to her stairs. At the top of her stairs, I'd come to her glass-paneled door. I'd knock on the door. She'd answer. "Hello, will you be my wife?" Husband and wife. And then we had a boy. I remember him, lying there in his crib, lying there grinning, his first Halloween and I made up a Halloween song for him.

> *Tomorrow, tomorrow*
> *Is good old Halloween*
> *And you're the prettiest Hobgoblin*
> *I ever have seen*

He's just lying there, grinning. My boy. It's late at night. And I'm waiting for my wife to get home from work and she's late and I'm sitting in the big chair in the living room, staring at the floor, sitting, waiting, not really doing anything. She's in the shower and we're screaming back and forth at each other and she opens up the shower door and she says, "Why don't you just leave me alone? I don't even like you anymore." And then she slams the door shut so hard that it shatters into a million bits and then she's standing there, in the water, bleeding, and then she's just standing there, crying. "You dumb bitch, you did it to yourself." And then I moved away. To look for work. I shouldn't have. But I did.

Harry's one-man show, *Pardon Me, I'm Having an Emotion*, as vividly performed as it was written, lured me into a world of solo performance that I hadn't considered. And it was Harry who introduced me to Rob. Whatever joy and wonder those two collaborative ventures instilled in me has remained with me for more than two decades. Both Harry and Rob were instrumental in my choice to fly solo. Their work continues to influence and guide me.

HARRY

We need each other—hell, we are each other! Really, don't you look at people and say, "That's me when I get older?" Or "That's me ten years ago." I see a part of myself in everyone I look at. Everyone. Black people, too. But it's harder. That's why there are black people—this wasn't meant to be easy! That's the cosmic joke—we're all the same soul packaged in different bodies. But gay people—we don't think anyone can identify with us. We feel left out of everything. When you hear "Rudolph the Red-Nosed Reindeer," who do you identify with? All of the other reindeer who used to laugh and call him names? No! You identify with Rudolph. Everybody does. We all have red noses. And when we fall in love with our shiny schnozollas—then we start flying! We gay people go out of our minds because we're afraid to go in them! Once we do, we often discover that wonderful little kid who lives inside of us! Like Peter Pan. Makes some grown-ups jealous. It's called Peter Envy.

Precious made a deal with the Zephyr to preview as long as we needed to in anticipation of opening sooner rather than later. We secured the theatre for one night a week indefinitely.

What the show needed, Precious and I agreed, was live music, a composer, a choreographer, a new ending, and to ditch the character of Temple, who now seemed a clever idea tacked on to the show rather than an organic piece of it.

It was seeming less and less like a solo show.

Did bringing in a musician and a choreographer make it less of a one-person show? Naw, I look at it as a technical aspect of the production, not unlike lighting or sound support. Solo requires collaboration. *The Porcelain Penelope Show* needed an onstage musician and some original music to allow the performer to reach new heights of theatricality. The entire proceedings would be energized by the dynamics that only a living, breathing musician could conjure.

Philip Solomon is a renaissance man of the theatre who created a score that provided an undercurrent for Snake Girl's revelations and Emma's confessions while providing Porcelain with the juice she needed to sparkle even more brightly. Even Sexy Mom had a subtle samba track that accompanied her juggling act. Only Grandma's monologue was delivered in silence, a deliberate choice since this was the character that was the most intensely dramatic of the lot. In fact, with Temple out of the "cast," Grandma now concluded the show and we needed to look at that, too.

Philip accompanied prerecorded music with drums and several percussion instruments. The sounds—assorted bells, xylophone, and even some special heavy breathing sounds, among them—gave the show an immediacy and energy. We also couldn't resist exploring the relationship between Porcelain and Duke (the name she chose for him). He became a perfect foil for Penelope's self-obsession.

PENELOPE

Say hello to Duke. He's my big brother. He goes everywhere with me. Don't you, Duke? He doesn't say much; he's shy. But that's okay because I like to talk!

Bringing in a choreographer could transform some monologues into quasi-musical numbers and simply provide more specific, focused movement in others. Kim Blank, one of Los Angeles' most respected choreographers, signed on and magic ensued. While I've worked with only a handful of choreographers, what immediately impressed me was Kim's desire to raise the stakes of the story being told. This is what good storytelling, on the page and on the stage, is all about. She was never interested in showing off her bag of tricks; rather, she was intent on finding the precise way in which movement could more honestly and emotionally drive the words.

While there was no question that we had assembled a stellar team of artists, it was my responsibility to see that the artistic forces came together for the show's next stage. The teamwork began about three weeks before the first preview at the Zephyr. How we collaborated varied, but it usually involved an initial meeting between Precious, Kim, and me. Precious and Kim would work together, then I'd take a look and offer my input.

In some instances, Kim and I chose a specific piece of music or a style—for example, the Snake Girl's number was in a generic fifties mode. Philip then added to the mix by tweaking the music we had suggested or by coming up with something he felt was better. When a particular dance didn't require perfectly timed steps, Philip created what I'd call a musical sound effect that evoked a mood. For instance, when the Snake Girl breaks away from her routine, a slightly eerie yet seductive blanket of sound plays along with her monologue. Because the collaboration between the four of us was so seamless, in many instances it became virtually impossible to say who made what choice(s) to make a particular section fly.

While the entertainment value of the piece was never in question, Precious and I never stopped questioning the purpose of the show. What is the theme? What are we trying to say? How do we want to affect the audience? Precious had not stopped writing—even though she wasn't consciously amassing new material for the show. I read everything she wrote with an eye to adding material if it would strengthen the story's themes.

The character we hadn't yet discussed was Precious Chong herself, who had been overshadowed by her multiple personas in the workshop production. While Porcelain Penelope was the character that overtook Precious with the greatest force, there was the authentic Precious who was always trying to emerge as a real person, not just as a theatrical construct. As we prepped for the second series of workshop performances, we looked at Precious' role in the proceedings. We pulled out that old acting axiom, posing the question: What was her intention?

She enters, reading from a book about snakes—one of those books that use symbolism to help you figure out your life. The audience immediately knows that she was trying to work something out (Precious, by the way, made the snake book. Not only did this save a few bucks, it increased her investment in the work. She had a task at hand—to make a book that worked along with the words. It was brightly colored but not without weight, literally and figuratively.)

It also seemed clear that she—Precious, the actress, who enters and exits in her street clothes—was playing these characters as a way to achieve a healthier self. While taking care of one's self cannot be the performer's main objective, one of the by-products of being an actor is gaining self-knowledge. The relentless perkiness of Porcelain, the defeated pain of the Snake Girl, the raw sexuality of Emma, the self-obsession of Sexy Mom, and the familial wound of Grandma were all aspects of Precious that she wanted to integrate, obliterate, or possibly exorcise.

We needed to provide the Precious character with a sense of closure. I don't mean that the show needed to be tied up neatly with a big bow. We didn't want to paint her as "healed" but definitely in the process of healing. I felt we needed what amounted to a closing number. Besides, the absence of Temple, who previously closed the show, left a significant hole. We looked at the material she had been working on. While it seemed to be written in Snake Girl's voice, it was also a bit more blatantly autobiographical than other material. In fact, remember the guy who sent the white roses? Read on.

PRECIOUS/SNAKE GIRL

Men think with their dicks. Went out with a snake. Blind date. Drove a black Corvette and lived in an ugly penthouse with a fish tank and a black leather couch. Hey, a snake. We should get married. The snake and his snake girl. Lay little snake eggs. He kissed like a fish, a piranha, a jellyfish, all limp hands, limp dick and I fell, fell, fell, for it. Hey, sing me a song and I'll give you a blow job. Note to self: do not sleep with them on the first date. Wait-a-minute, darlin', I'm still kicking. I'll write a tell-all

40

book, I'll work for charities. I mean, Heather Mills got a Beatle
and she's missing a goddamn limb I will not be ignored.
Ahhhhhhhhssssssssssssssssssssswwwwwoooossssssssssswooooooo.
Wo-wo-wow, man! This little girl act is only going to get me by
for so long. The beast in me, well it wants it, it wants it, it wants
to fuck everything or everyone in sight. You are a dirty girl! Ah,
you little cunt, I will not igahhhhhhhhhssssssssssssssnnnnnnnnnn-
aaaaaakkkkkkkkewwwooooooooman. I don't make a dent. I
want to make a dent. Gotta go to the doctor. Health insurance.
Honey, work in a hotel they give you all the benefits. The path
of no benefits. The path of least resistance. Work it out onstage.
How boring to work it out onstage. Ouch. Keep a lid on it.
"They say it's only a paper moon." I'm gettin myself a toy boy,
Harry's dead and it's time to have some fun. Hey, I always hated
throwing up. My mom would say if you just let yourself be sick
you'll feel better. But I couldn't, I couldn't do it. Couldn't let go.
If I would just scream loud enough, just cry hard enough. I did
finally let it hurl that night at my parents' house. They thought it
was food poisoning but it I knew it was them, me. I couldn't do
it anymore. I'll be this, you be that. The good daughter role, the
little girl act, was making me sick. Chucked up my guts and
then quit working for my mom to get out of this shadow. Need
to make a dent. My daddy got busted by the Feds and now I'm
all alone. Please, Mr. Ashcroft, let my daddy go I don't even like
pot, I like Starbucks. All my life I waited for them to get caught.
I wanted them to be straight, I wanted them to get busted and
be normal and be like everyone else I . . . Wait a minute you
can't do this to me, I'm just a little girl. Fuck you, I'm a
Republican and I'm proud. Oowwwyou'rehurtinme—ssnaaa-
keeewommannnnnnnnn. I heard about P. Diddy. In the dream, I
wanted him to take me seriously, so I called him Sean. Do you
even count if you're not famous? I want, I want. Be clear about
what you want. Hello, Los Angeles! Can you hear me? I'm care-
less with my heart. I'm reckless with my pussy. He said all the
right things. Real. I want something real. Real, real, real, real,
real, real. Give me something real. Instead of driving around
and trying not to bounce checks. I don't know why I do it, huh?

Right. A true artist. Fuck that. I wanna be Kate Hudson. I wanna marry a rock star. I did it all wrong. Hello, Los Angeles. Wake up motherfuckers! I don't make a dent, right?

As Kim put it, "In terms of the script, this piece was in process more than the others. I hit upon the idea of staging the piece as a snake-shaped path or a mandala. Precious/Snake Girl began her monologue on the circumference of a sort of imaginary coil, or spiral, and as she spoke, conveying her conscious thoughts, the voices of the various characters we had seen in the show would emerge and interrupt her. As the characters asserted themselves, some of their thematic movements or dance steps emerged as well. A struggle seemed to ensue with the character before she was able to shed the character.

"Precious/Penelope would proceed, winding her way from the outer circumference, into smaller circumferences, getting interrupted by each of the characters, finally finding herself center stage, center spiral, for the last words of the monologue."

This was different from the numbers that were staged very deliberately, and Kim remembers that we agreed to "let this last monologue have a less choreographed, more organic shape, more of a path to walk than a dance to perform. This contrast also seemed to work with the theme that was developing in the overall piece. Technically, I thought it would serve the actress as well, letting the movement come from the words more than being imposed and tied to them. We had time constraints in our rehearsal process, which made it desirable to keep the structure simple and the movement uncomplicated."

While I didn't admit it immediately, I saw this final monologue as the equivalent of "Rose's Turn" from *Gypsy.*

When somebody told Jim Pickett, after seeing me perform his one-man play *Dream Man,* that the experience "was like seeing Ethel Merman sing 'Rose's Turn,'" Jim thought I'd be insulted.

"Honey," I said, "I consider it a supreme compliment."

"Rose's Turn" is essentially a searing monologue with music, loaded with dramatic twists and turns, climaxing more than once before a devastating conclusion. The dynamics—words by Steven Sondheim, music by Jule Styne—provides a valuable lesson for all soloists.

I was confident that Kim's sensitivity, coupled with Philip's music, would bring the show to a dazzling conclusion. The last number was not as blazingly theatrical as the other "dances," but it was far more abstract and emotionally complex. The piece took place after the show within the show had climaxed and ended. Precious had taken her final bows and had put on her street clothes. It was as if she was alone in the theatre, working out some new material.

Because this second ending was, by choice, after the show's ostensible climax, it ran the risk of being anticlimactic. We had to rebuild to a second crescendo, on an emotional level rather than a visual one, since the stage was more neutral in terms of lighting and ambience. It was also more than seven minutes. We were determined to make it work without shortening it. While the guidelines for writing a solo show are less strict than they would be for writing a two-act play, you do need to know where your show peaks. From the moment you walk onstage, you are on a path to that moment.

After the movement was semi-set, it was time to direct the acting. That's where I came in, attempting to make sense of the entire creation. It was a stylistic leap and we knew it.

There were also some strictly cosmetic changes. The floating door frame had no character; it needed to pop. "Pink fur!" Precious suggested. In the midst of her intensely colorful wardrobe, an unadorned door frame seemed out of place. Since her dressing table was covered with leftover pink fur, adding remnants of it to the door frame made sense.

On the day we were loading into the Zephyr, I turned off Melrose onto the side street where we routinely parked and noticed a handsome, middle-aged man lifting a door frame festooned in hot pink fur out of a pickup truck. It was Precious' dad, Tommy Chong. He maneuvered the unwieldy frame like a professional stagehand. By the time I parked the car and walked to the theatre entrance, he and Precious were in the midst of a discussion about the wacky door.

Precious introduced us and he gave me a firm handshake and looked me right in the eye, a refreshingly un-Hollywood approach. I was impressed with the obvious joy he was experiencing by helping his daughter get her show on the boards. The three of us collaborated on the placement of the door, checking the sight lines and determining the door's stability.

"Cheech and I performed here," he said.

"You're kidding!?" I said, delighted.

He and Cheech had participated in some comedy-sketch show at the Zephyr decades prior. Actors—and Precious is no exception—glom onto these delicious tidbits and believe that the magic coincidences are a sign of good luck. And I agree. Tommy knew that we had a big day ahead of us so he took off and we began making the adjustments required by moving from the rehearsal studio to the Zephyr stage. The work we'd done at the Elephant was not applicable, since the Zephyr has a thrust stage and Precious would be playing to three areas surrounding her. Kim, of course, had taken this into consideration when she designed the movement, but there are always adjustments to be made when you are actually in the space.

Don't fight it is my motto. Let the changes inspire you. Most spaces, especially those that house solo work, come with kinks and quirks. Use 'em. Even the space provides an opportunity for collaboration. One of the aisles in the theatre leads to the light booth. I used it as a surprise entrance for the Hooligan character, who has supposedly been watching the show with the audience.

Precious adapted to the space naturally. The numbers had to be opened up since they were originally staged presentationally. Because the final monologue was brand-new and more abstract in feel, it took a lot of time and energy to bring to life.

Gary, the theatre's proprietor, did the lighting plot. As is often the case with a solo show that shares the space with one or more other shows (some of which might take precedence), we are usually at the mercy of what fixed lighting is available. It forces a heightened creativity and I've simply come to accept it. Remember that the lighting is designed to make the story you are telling more vivid and understandable.

In November 2002, we did four preview performances without making any drastic changes from one performance to another. Previews are often dressed-up rehearsals, and that was certainly the case with this show. Material that hasn't undergone the luxury of an extended rehearsal process needs to settle and can't be evaluated without several performances. I didn't want to rush the process.

I was never entirely certain that the audience grasped what we intended them to understand in the final piece. Precious was vocally and physically rejecting the personas, essentially killing them off one by one. She was trying to find her own voice and tell her own story without their getting in the way. It was certainly vocally and textually entertaining, and I don't think anyone got bored although it did require that audiences stretch their attention span because the show lasted nearly an hour.

I'm convinced that audiences get things subliminally; they don't necessarily have to be bluntly told the theme of the show. In fact, it is unfair to spell out the theme. While that might be appropriate in a newspaper article, the theatre audience wants to experience the story with the hero of the show. Allow the audience to discover along with you as you move through the performance piece. The ending was daring and challenging for performer and audience, and we kept it through the previews and the Zephyr run.

One of the reasons for previews is to avoid being reviewed too early. Eventually, however, reviews are needed to bring in an audience. Precious was great at promoting the show—making and distributing nifty flyers and posters. I helped with publicity and the two of us managed to make a dent in the overcrowded LA entertainment market. This is an aspect of solo that some artists might resent doing or even consider demeaning. The simple truth is that, with few exceptions, most solo shows don't have a budget to hire a publicist.

I consider self-promotion one of the by-products of tackling a one-person show. Call it an exercise in self-esteem building. It's an extension of artistic ownership that gives you some autonomy. On the rare occasion that one of my shows had a press agent, it was unlikely that they could strategize a way to sell my show better than I could. Take responsibility for your creation.

That said, if you aren't good at selling yourself, it may be a talent you'll need to hone, and hiring a professional may help provide you with the necessary tools. Again, collaboration is key, but don't relinquish your responsibility to bring in an audience; like it or not, it is expected of the soloist who hasn't hit the mainstream.

"In most cases," according to Highways' administrative director Mary Milelzcik, "Highways co-partners with artists in producing performances. Therefore, artists are expected to take some responsibility for getting an audience. Co-producing means that Highways and the artist have to work together." Or collaborate. "Larger theatres have their own PR person or department. Most small or medium-sized theatres (both for-profit and nonprofit) are understaffed and the PR person wears many hats. Competition is fierce; it seems like everyone in Los Angeles has a solo show.

"Artists have the responsibility to provide the theatre with clearly written press release information, press kits, and good-quality production photos in a timely manner in order to get the best press possible."

Because many solo performers don't have a clue how to represent themselves, Milelzcik created Arts Asylum to address some of these issues. She conducts marketing/PR workshops and does individual consultations with artists to teach them "how to market themselves without being overwhelmed or going broke in the process."

Some of her tips "for the performer to make promotion easier" include the following:

- Don't be a drama queen.
- Treat people with respect.
- Be honest. We can't fix a problem that we don't know about.
- Create a long bio and keep it updated. From that, create a one-page paragraph and a two-liner.

- Make sure your PR accurately portrays your performance. Critics get mean when they feel that they have been misled.

- Create and maintain a good database of press and people interested in your work and keep it updated.

- Develop a relationship with press people. Don't be afraid to call them. Most of them are very nice.

- Don't underestimate the importance of a great photo—interesting, clear, and related to the show.

- At the end of the run, thank everyone who did anything for you during your production.

We enjoyed the luxury of previews for *The Porcelain Penelope Show* at the Zephyr. Even though we technically hadn't opened, the show attracted a very Hollywood crowd. In addition to her parents (who faithfully attended several performances) there were other show-biz types including actors and actresses Precious had worked with. And, yes, Cheech Marin showed up one night.

The response was enthusiastic. Everyone agreed that Precious was a dazzler and she wasn't putting on "just another solo show." The only criticism from her mom was to return the Dolce & Gabana leopard trenchcoat that she'd borrowed for Emma's costume (without telling her). A costume that was casually thrown on the floor by the Stripper Who Talks during the striptease.

Finding a new coat with any kind of glamour quotient wasn't easy so we settled for basic black until Precious spotted a red leather number in a Melrose shop a few doors down from the theatre.

"Should I get it?" she asked, describing it to me. We were in her dressing room, chatting before the show one night. "It's red leather. $100."

I opted for frugality.

This happened to be on a night when Tommy, her dad, was attending the preview. The majority of the audience was already in the house, and Tommy was about to go in as I brought Precious down from the dressing room. Her entrance was from the same door that the audience used, maintaining the conceit that she was entering from the street. It was after 8:00.

The minute she saw her dad, who was poised to walk through the door, she whispered, "Psssst. Dad." He stopped in his tracks.

"Can I borrow $100? I don't have any credit cards with me and there's a coat I need for the show."

Without blinking, he pulled out a hundred-dollar bill.

"It will only take a minute," she said and was on her way before I knew what was going on.

The preshow tape played. Tommy and I exchanged "Is she nuts?" looks as he entered the theatre and found a seat. Within a few minutes, she reappeared, breathless, with Emma's new coat in her hot little hands.

"How do I get it onstage?" she asked.

"Carry it on like you're bringing in a new costume for one of your characters. It will work."

It did work, and the scarlet coat proved to be fabulous, especially framed in pink fur on her entrance. The moral of the story? It's nice to have Tommy Chong as your dad when you want to indulge in an extravagant costume.

There were more contributions from Papa Chong. It would have been ridiculously naïve of me not to anticipate that her father would be giving Precious notes about the performances that he saw. She told me about some of them, saying that she had no intention of listening to a second director. Even though I trusted her, I still felt a bit threatened. At a particular moment in a performance I was watching from the back row, I realized Tommy was sitting directly in front of me and Precious was in our line of vision. I thought to myself, melodramatically, "He's come between us."

It's true that I covet my parental role. It's part of what makes a good director, but it's also not to be overplayed. In truth, Tommy wasn't crossing any boundaries. I was just overdramatizing the potential for conflict but it never happened.

The show opened for the critics in December of 2003. But guess what? They didn't come. Press releases were mailed, phone calls were made, and follow-up was thorough. They did not come.

When there is negative press (or no press) or lukewarm press response, it is more challenging for the solo performer and director to avoid taking it on personally. With a cast that consists of other performers, there's a built-in support system. Your options for commiserating are limited when it's just you, your director, and maybe a few techies (who may or may not care).

When you are a soloist—onstage, in the dressing room, on the plane en route, in the hotel room—you are often alone. In this example, and many others, you'll see that the solo show is a metaphor for many things involving self: self-respect, self-love, self-acceptance, self-esteem, self-control, self-confidence. But not *all* things—please avoid self-obsession and self-indulgence.

Thankfully, the word of mouth was strong enough to capture a healthy audience, but to be unacknowledged by the press was disappointing—and a bit confusing. Precious has a sturdy reputation as an actress in LA and has been consistently lauded for her theatrical outings. My work has been reviewed with great respect for thirty years. I assumed the combo would attract every critic in town.

Not one. Attempting to figure out the odd inner workings of the press is futile, but that doesn't stop anyone from trying. It's true that solo shows (especially in the entertainment capital of the world) have been given a bad rap because so many of them are pumped up pleas for attention and void of any artistic merit. It is also true that Hollywood notoriously eschews entertainment that is about the Industry (which may have been miscommunicated in the press release).

In the initial release, I had written the following description:

The Porcelain Penelope Show, with Precious Chong playing "the cutest little girl in the whole wide world" and starring a cast of Hollywood show people (all played by Chong) . . . In her solo debut, the actress creates a New Vaudeville revue with a lineup that includes child star Porcelain Penelope and her fractured selves, a bevy of has-beens and wanna-bes, including: Emma, the Stripper Who Talks; The Juggling Sexiest Mom in the World; Hitler the Emcee; The Hooligan; Grandma Edna, the Incredible Shrinking Woman; Snake Girl, the Backup Dancer; and the Talking Vagina. A new theatrical phenomenon making waves in Los Angeles, New Vaudeville combines a number of show-biz traditions including juggling, burlesque, stand-up, and many of the various theatrical permutations simply labeled as "performance."

If it wasn't the press release, was it too close to the *Winona* experience? Was I doing too many shows? Am I a has-been? It's all about me, isn't it?

There were no answers, of course, just neurotic speculation. After several weeks, the *LA Weekly* finally showed up and, although it was a very intelligent and favorable review, it didn't make you run to the phone to reserve seats:

> Under Michael Kearns' direction, Chong is a bundle of feverish energy, her near-constant movement distracting at first but later serving as an effective counterpoint in her closing monologue. There is nothing particularly novel about these characters, eccentric though some are, but Chong's observations are incisive, and they blend with her skilled presentation of the show's various personalities.

While a rave might have sweetened the experience, this was a solid review and we knew it. It was to her credit that she didn't let up in terms of getting the word out on her own, securing the show's good reputation on the street. I arranged for her to do a radio interview on our local Pacifica station—every little bit helps.

Then I received a call from Danielle at Highways (who had seen the first performance at the Elephant). She was teaming up three women who were new on the performance scene for a weekend gig under the umbrella title *Contenders*. She invited Precious to be on the bill.

Highways has been one of the country's leading presenters of solo work for the past fifteen years. In addition to yours truly, artists whose work is tied to Highways include Tim Miller, Holly Hughes, Dan Kwong, Keith Antar-Mason, Lypsyncha, Alec Mapa, Noel Alumit, and countless others. In many respects, a weekend appearance at Highways (even as part of a trio of performers) was more prestigious for a soloist than several weeks at the Zephyr.

This made absolutely no sense whatsoever to Precious, who was primarily a gal of the theatre. I'm not sure she'd ever been to Highways and she certainly didn't have more than a passing interest in solo work. Even though she knew I wouldn't steer her in the wrong direction, she resisted from the get-go. In a phone message to me, she haughtily announced, "I'm an actress, not a performance artist. What is a performance artist anyway?" She was responding to a press release she'd read, presumably out of fear that this gig would somehow diminish her status as a serious actress. About two minutes later, another message, saying that she was sorry for being "difficult." But it didn't stop there.

There were slightly facetious comments about a meeting she had with the other two women on the bill a couple of weeks before the performance. "One of them talks about working in a San Francisco store that sells sex toys," Precious said. "Her piece is called *Novice Fucker.*" Understandably, she was worried that the characters might not play out of context, a concern I shared with her. She would perform bits of Porcelain, Snake Girl, and the loud-mouthed Vagina.

What I wasn't thrilled about was another tech rehearsal, creating lighting from scratch. No one knows the tediousness of a tech rehearsal—setting the sound cues and light cues while the technicians sometimes seem to be moving in slow motion. The tech invariably takes twice as long as expected so that everyone is on edge, especially if there is a show within hours.

On the day that *Contenders* opened, a big photo of Precious (by herself) appeared in the *LA Weekly* with words of praise about each of the individual artists. It was the best press we'd gotten thus far. "Precious Chong comes by her vaudevillian chops honestly (yes, that

Chong) . . . For this gig Chong has selected the chapter of her one-woman show in which dear Porcelain finds herself facing off—and strapping on—her big, hairy and talking vagina."

Precious finally acknowledged that the Highways stint imbued *The Porcelain Penelope Show* with a certain stature that it had not previously achieved. In retrospect, she admitted that her resistance was entirely because she "didn't want to be on the same bill with other women."

After twelve weeks at the Zephyr, Precious was scheduled to go off to Ventura, California, to join a cast of (other) women onstage, appearing in *Dancing at Lughnasa* with Bonnie Franklin, Stephanie Zimbalist, and Susan Clark, directed by Jenny Sullivan.

In the weeks preceding the final performances, Precious and I discussed the possibility of doing some shows in Ventura (on her night off) or remounting *The Porcelain Penelope Show* when she finished the *Lughnasa* run. As she was readying herself to make the transition from working solo show to working in an ensemble, there wasn't much time for writing.

However, when Tommy Chong was busted by the Feds for selling bongs on the Web, making international headlines, she had no choice. Write, she must. As an artist, she had no choice but to persevere.

Exercise/Collaboration

Bring in a trusted friend—someone with some artistic sensibility. You can make this person your director or your coach or your consultant. Your collaborator. But team up with someone on the work you've done so far. Obviously, for the purposes of this exercise, choose someone who is going to be supportive.

This should be a conversation, a collaboration about the work, not a judgment call. Does your teammate get it? Is anything confusing? Are there suggestions to make it clearer? More alive? Is it emotional? Is it self-indulgent? Does it need any simple effects to give it more juice? A prop? A hint of a costume? Collaborate. Realize that you need another eye and two more ears (at least).

If you argue a bit, fine. But keep it fairly simple and short; it needn't last more than forty-five minutes or so.

Chapter 3 Checklist

- Are you able to let go of your control queen voice in order to be part of a collaboration?
- Are you doing a solo show instead of going to therapy?
- Do you have the qualities of a team player that are necessary for a healthy collaboration?
- Are all the elements of your show (music, set, lighting, choreography) serving the overall purpose: to tell a story?
- Collaboration requires listening. Do you know when to shut up?
- Are you able to be self-promoting?
- Are you setting yourself up to be too reliant on reviews to bring in an audience?

4 Perseverance

What would you do if you couldn't fail? What if there was no such thing as rejection? What if every experience—good or bad—served you somehow?

Alec Mapa

If the news of her father's arrest was surreal for me, what must it have been for Precious? It made headlines in Hollywood. While reports varied, it was certain that the authorities confiscated about $120,000 in proceeds from the sales of pipes and glass bongs. The crackdown was part of a national government drug sweep by the government called "Operation Pipe Dreams," overseen by John Ashcroft. Chong's company, Nice Dreams, was one of several facing illegal drug charges.

Precious made the transition from portraying family histrionics in Ireland (*Dancing at Lughnasa*) to the real-life drama of the Chong family in Hollywood with her usual combination of grace and good humor as revelation upon revelation exploded in her head.

I don't recall one particular moment when we decided that the next installment of *The Porcelain Penelope Show* would be more directly autobiographical. It honestly felt organic to the process. It was as if the real-life events, as painful as they were, somehow fed the themes of the unraveling story being told by Precious and her band of characters. She persevered with a ferocity that is usually associated with Olympics-hopeful athletes.

Thinking things out was not part of her emotional state. She moved forward with great intensity, intuitively and instinctively. Even though it was surely difficult, she was flowing. The material would flow and the performance would flow in ways it never had before.

We were approached by Harris Smith, an impresario who takes enormous pride in his West Hollywood cabaret space, the Masquers Cabaret, to do a run there in May, and we thought that a new space would give the show a necessary goose (as if the juicy headlines weren't enough). So this version of *The Porcelain Penelope Show* was influenced both by the venue and by real-life events.

Tommy's case, like most court cases, dragged on for months. At this stage of the interminable process, there were more unknowns than knowns. We attempted to stay in the moment. There is a point in any show's evolution, and especially one that isn't set, when you must let go of any notion that you can *make* things happen. Instead, you must *allow* things to happen, accept them, and use them accordingly.

We didn't inhibit the writing process by making adjustments based on the new space. Precious had booked it on her own and I trusted her instincts. She warned me that it was small. Reworking some of the material, we kept in mind that the attention span of the audience would not hold as long in a cabaret setting as it did in the theatre. Grandma, for instance, needed to be trimmed considerably.

We also knew that the space allowed a more unrestrained freedom in terms of sheer theatricality that simply doesn't feel appropriate in a theatre setting. We could play a bit more, be a bit more cheeky. We gave Porcelain a new song that was probably the most blatantly political addition to the revised show. There's a scene in *Whatever Happened to Baby Jane* in which Bette Davis, as the demented child star who never grew up, sings a ditty called, "I've Written a Letter to Daddy." Precious rewrote the lyrics, pleading with Attorney General John Ashcroft to "release" her dad.

PORCELAIN PENELOPE

Okay, my next song is dedicated to my Papa.
(*She sings*)

> I wrote a letter to Mr. Ashcroft
> Please don't lock up my Dad
> I promise, Mr. Ashcroft, he'll be different

> *No more Pope of Dope, won't you be glad*
> *I'm sorry, Miss Mary Beth Buchanan*
> *That Chong's Bong's made you so mad*
> *Was* Up in Smoke *really that bad?*

(*Speaking*)
Dear Mr. Ashcroft: My Daddy is very sorry that he made you mad. I told him what you said, Mr. Ashcroft, that only dopes smoke dope. He knows better now and won't ever do it again. Cross his heart and hope to die, stick a needle in his eye. All my love, Penelope. X, X, X.

We were raising the personal stakes of the show. Even though the intimate nature of the material was unsettling for Precious (despite the fact that it was comedic), she persevered where others with less strength and confidence would have crumbled. One of her greatest fears was that she would be accused of exploiting the situation. Even though we knew that we had been working on *The Porcelain Penelope Show* for a year, would the public and press accuse her of taking advantage of her father's arrest to enhance her career?

Before tackling a solo show, Mark Travis warns, "You will be regarded by some as being self-centered, self-aggrandizing, self-pitying, and on and on. Accept it, not as truth, but as an understandable reaction. Others will be jealous, impatient, overly encouraging, demanding, critical, etc. This all comes with the territory. You need a thick skin while at the same time allowing yourself to be vulnerable enough to do the work. It will test you."

There was also the very real possibility that her show could potentially antagonize the authorities. This was not just us being paranoid. The "Operation Pipe Dreams" team had been tracking Tommy for over a year. Would it be so unlikely that they would check out his daughter's show? Although we never had any real indication that the authorities did check out the show, she used it as a recurring theme in the text, suggesting to the audience that she was "being followed."

During the show's May run at the Masquers, Tommy pleaded guilty in his Pittsburgh court appearance. When Penelope apologizes to the audience for her dad not being able to make it to the show, she tagged the line with, "He's pleading guilty in Pittsburgh." And while Tommy's actions outside the federal courthouse may have played well on the nightly news, it would prove to be detrimental to his case down the line. He jokingly told the media that he might put the criminal case in his next movie with Cheech Marin. The U.S. Attorney's office pointed to this statement as a lack of remorse on Chong's part, said he was making light of the case and might seek to exploit it for money. Everyone felt certain that he'd receive a community services sentence or house arrest. But it was all speculation.

"We cannot predict," I said. "We've got to stay in the moment."

Fortunately, we had our work cut out for us and couldn't spend too much time considering every possible scenario that might (or might not) occur and eventually affect the show. The cabaret venue was a challenge to be dealt with sooner than later. Each venue comes with a laundry list of dos and don'ts. Since this was a café that served dinner and was booked with back-to-back acts, we had some major rules to obey.

The Masquers Cabaret is a quaint little club that tries to recapture some of the old Hollywood. The walls are decorated with huge George Hurrell photographs of movie stars of yesteryear. Red leather booths line the walls and, in a nod to the seventies, a disco ball hangs from the ceiling. It actually suited Porcelain's shenanigans, even though the stage was only about ten feet deep and twenty feet wide (about a fourth the size of the Zephyr playing area).

Harris charged an hourly rate for tech rehearsals, so we were forced to use our time wisely. Several days before our first performance there, we went in and took measurements of the stage (half of which was taken up by a piano), in order to reblock it in the rehearsal studio.

The most exciting element was our choice to bring the "acts" into the audience. This would require some additional input from Kim, readjusting the movements for Penelope, Snake Girl, and Emma.

Since there was no follow spot, we improvised with one of those big industrial flashlights. The light and sound person followed Emma, the stripper, around. At one point, she wound up in a doorway, draped in burgundy red velvet, captured in the too-bright glare of a make-believe spotlight. And, of course, Emma deserved that disco ball in all its bygone glory.

EMMA

Sex Fantasy Number Two: I'm a nanny or a housemaid in an English manor and I am forced to have sex with the Lord or Duke. It happens in an antique armoire. Don't ask me why.

Many of the adjustments could not be fully anticipated in the rehearsal room setting so we were madly restaging, practically until showtime. Because the stage was narrow and wide, we had to place the "dressing room" next to the "onstage" area. Previously upstage (and sharing equal length of the playing area), the dressing area was now stage right of the raised stage and claustrophobic.

This was further complicated by time constrictions, since part of the playing area was also a path from the bar/kitchen area to the dining room, so we weren't allowed to set up until everyone was served.

Precious' friend Amy (the one who made the door frame) was again helping us with the tech rehearsal and I realized that we could incorporate her into the show. Adding another body to a set that was already crowded may seem downright dumb but the space restrictions also made it more difficult for Precious to deal with props and costumes by herself. It made sense to have Amy play her dresser (if she wanted to).

Would it, however, make sense emotionally? We had to give her a role that increased the stakes of the story line. If we cast her as the dresser for Precious/Penelope and her multiple personalities, it seemed likely that she would be treated in the same way that the star treated Duke, her musician. Because Philip had other work conflicts, we'd been through a number of onstage musicians. Our present Duke was Tahmus Rounds, who was also a wonderful actor.

We made Tahmus and Amy a secret couple, united in their disdain for the diva who wouldn't allow them to speak. If discovered by the Precious/Penelope character, this romance would drive her insane since she was not exactly lucky in love.

While the Precious/Penelope character's unsuccessful love life is not spelled out, it is referenced by the Sexy Mom, and both Snake Girl and Emma reflect on being unlucky in love themselves.

We restaged the opening of the show with Tahmus and Amy making eyes at each other as they prepared for the arrival of their mistress, who was late because of an audition for a television commercial. At one point, Amy held one of the costumes up to her to check out how she'd look in it and I was struck by the similarity to the opening of Genet's *The Maids*. I wish I could say that I was clever enough to have made that choice intentionally.

When Precious/Penelope arrived, the two characters (living in the one actress) had a heated conversation right outside the entrance into the Masquers. She entered, frantically pulling bobby pins out of her hair.

At this juncture, the Hooligan was still in the show. At one point, when the Talking Vagina wouldn't shut up, Penelope fled the theatre, did a quick change, and returned as the Hooligan who rubs shoulders, literally, with the audience.

After the light/sound man tossed the Hooligan out of the club for his obnoxious behavior, and since Penelope hadn't returned, Tahmus and Amy decided to take the opportunity to bask in the spotlight. Precious has multitalented friends and associates. Since Amy and Tahmus are expert jugglers, I had them do a dazzling juggling bit.

Back in her Penelope drag, she quietly entered as they basked in the audience's undivided attention. She placed herself in the aisle, observed for a few minutes, and then let out a blood-curdling scream as if witnessing a murder.

Admittedly, the addition of two characters who are interacting is a bit of a cheat on the established one-person format. How did we justify it? The time actually taken up by the dresser and Duke (not including when he's functioning as a musician) was probably less than 5 percent of the show. They were also nonspeaking (yeah, I know, so was Helen Keller in *The Miracle Worker*). Perhaps most important, it was done to support the material and the performer. If at some point I felt like we really crossed the line and the show had to be restructured as a play, I would have been open to that. At this juncture, however, I felt that we were simply taking artistic liberties.

Because the work with Precious was in such good shape and so gratifying, I felt I had the energy to work on a second piece simultaneously. Seth Cutler had approached me about working with him on a solo piece. He had been my student and I had directed him in *Trafficking in Broken Hearts* several years prior so I knew how utterly diligent he was. I also knew he had a very specific sense of humor—part Jewish, part gay, part Borscht Belt.

He had several pages of material in varying stages of development. What I wanted, I found; there was a character there and a show could potentially evolve. Not afraid to work, we began fleshing out the isolated bits and putting them into an order that made some dramatic sense. Seth was ambitious but realistic and was looking at doing a few performances in a modest and inexpensive setting to try it out. But even that requires money, energy, and a lot of hard work.

Seth is also a person with a lot of people in his life who love and support him. I knew that this might be a perfectly justifiable experiment that he might get out of his system. I'm not minimizing it nor am I minimizing my role. I took it very seriously, but I suspected it might be the obligatory one-man show experience that every actor feels the need to experience.

His show, *Beyond the Song*, concerned his character Jon-Michael's urgent quest for self-improvement. The setting (the theatre, in this case) was an aerobics studio that served the environmental conceit. It was the location of the Going Beyond seminar. To celebrate graduating, Jon-Michael makes his final presentation to audience members who, in the show's conceit, are his Going Beyond peers.

Relying on lyrics from his favorite songs to express himself (some of which were also in his mind and played "live" on a CD player), Jon-Michael went through various stages to achieve self-esteem. Unlike the singer-actress who wanted to use Streisand songs, this character was obsessed with song lyrics; in fact, he often spoke in familiar lyrics.

Because the obsession with song lyrics was the character's obsession, not the actor's, it was artistically viable.

Each of the seminar's topics provided Jon-Michael with an opportunity to show how he'd used each of the seminar topics to improve himself. Among them were First Love, Red Flags, Wildest Dreams, The Next, and Trauma.

Seth's show was on its feet in the spring, bringing the material to life, but also pointing out the need for a lot of restructuring. At one point in May, I advised him to set the workshop performance dates for August.

"We did not actually start on the acting rehearsals until July," Seth recalled. "I thought, 'Oh my God, August is four weeks away and we just began the acting rehearsals.' I felt like I needed more time."

"No matter what the opening date is, you'll feel like you need more time," I told him.

He was very well prepared, working like a demon. Because of time constraints and the expense of renting a rehearsal space, I expect the writer-performer to do a lot of work on his own. If I'm working on an hourly basis, this is imperative. But even if we've agreed on a set fee for my services, I do not want to spend an inordinate amount of time while the actor-writer goes through the baby steps.

The soloist must be willing to do an extensive amount of homework in between our meetings if we are to progress without wasting time in the rehearsal studio. I have no desire to baby-sit while a writer does rewrites. Nor do I want to hand-hold while an acting moment is explored.

I make very strong and specific suggestions about where I think the writing and acting need to go. I then expect the writer-performer to work his butt off in between meetings,

I'm also not interested in someone simply delivering my notes. Spin from my notes. Contradict me. Enhance my notes. Bring in something better than what I suggested. But do your homework!

Just as Seth was about to begin his run of workshop performances, Precious was embarking on a trip to Vancouver where she would debut yet another version of *The Porcelain Penelope Show*. At this point, it was astounding how quickly we could pull things together. She had written an extraordinary monologue about doing a commercial in which she had to put herself in a dangerous situation, physically and emotionally.

PRECIOUS

I find out about the bust from my mom. I call the house, my parents' house, that morning and some man answers, "Chong residence." I laugh because he sounds so formal and I think it's one of my brother's friends joking around and then I say, "Hi, is my mom there?" "Mrs. Chong can't talk right now. Can she call you back?" I'm in Best Buy, which is a big appliance store in the States, and I'm buying a tape recorder. I'm in rehearsals for *Dancing at Lughnasa* at the time and I'm workin' on my Irish dialect. So my mom calls my cell phone. "They raided our house, Precious." It turns out they've been following my whole family for a year. I mean, maybe my phone is being tapped. Maybe they are following me. I imagine them following me. Two men. Straight. Straight-laced. Cute in a preppy way. One a Colin Farrell type. The other, more Benicio Del Toro. By the book. They both fall in love with me as they follow me from commercial audition to commercial audition. Changing costumes in my car—into my casual mom clothes, quirky mom, upscale casual, office upscale, sexy secretary, construction worker. Maybe they even came to *The Porcelain Penelope Show* in LA and I would be like Karen Finley. Persecuted for my art, threatening the white male status quo and yet showing a vulnerability and dedication that is irresistible to one of those DEA guys. Those DEA guys are in love with me. Seeing me sacrifice my body and soul for my art. The time I audition for the Burger King UK spot. "You have to be willing to show your bare ass at the audition," Pam, my agent, tells me over the phone. "Don't go if you have a problem with nudity." I literally slate my bare ass at the audition. "Hi, I'm Precious Chong." Close-up on bare bottom. Then I slate it at the callback. I always get the weird ones. The next day Pam calls me and tells me I'm the director's first choice. Just don't treat me like I'm a piece of ass. The spot is of a woman running through the streets in a hospital gown, hooked up to an IV and rolling an oxygen tank. Take after take after take and the oxygen tank is awkward and keeps hitting me on the ankle. The director is young and ironic and detached. He doesn't care. I want people to kiss my ass. I want people to rush up to me in between takes with a chair, wrap me in a blanket and hand me water and Diet Coke and tell me in hushed ones how brave I am and how grateful they are that I am here. Don't these people know who I am? Don't they know that I am the daughter of a counterculture drug icon currently being persecuted by a right-wing Christian government? I mean, this is big. Where are those DEA guys? My future husbands. How can they bear to watch me being treated so shabbily? Why aren't they flying out of their Chrysler Le Baron and rushing up to the crew flashing badges and taking me away. I feel like Frances Farmer. I'm having a hard time getting the oxygen tank up the curb. It's not really built for speed. I get one good take where I almost knock this poor extra out. I must look crazy. I'm crazy. I feel like I'm losing control. And I do. Just as I make it to the other side of the street, the oxygen tank spins out of control, knocking my ankles and shin black and blue. Everyone rushes toward me. "Are you okay? Are you okay?" I'm going to be brave. I'm going to be a trooper. I'm a professional. But the attention gets to me. Finally, they are paying attention. The tears come and my face crinkles up like it used to when I was little—five years old, eleven, fifteen, twenty-three, thirty-two. Okay, fine, I'm a crier. Why? Why do I do this? Why am I doing this? Why am I even telling this story, here and now, to you? Why do I care? Why do I want so badly to be heard? My voice. My point of view. It's all crap. What I'm writing—it's all caca doodle doo.

She had performed the piece at Comedy Union's women's night and it was certainly appropriate material for the direction in which the show was heading. At this point, we introduced yet another side of her:

Precious, the Stand-Up Comic. The immediacy of stand-up better suited the up-to-the-minute material that we could, literally, rewrite an hour before showtime.

For the Canadian run, there were other considerations. Many of her relatives lived in Canada, including the Grandma who was a compelling part of the show. Because the new stand-up monologue was long and because she did not want to risk hurting her beloved grandma in any way, we cut her.

In truth, what the Grandma character provided—the passing on of physical quirks and ticks, not to mention emotional roots, from generation to generation—was not necessary to move this revised story along.

I must confess that both of us tended to keep the Grandma piece because it provided Precious with a real Meryl Streep moment in which she could act her head off. And it did stop the show. Even though it may be gratifying for the performer-writer and director, it is not necessarily a good thing to have a Big Moment that, over time, will likely become very self-conscious. And, besides, who wants to hurt their grandma?

This is, understandably, a stumbling block for many soloists who are writing autobiography. They become absolutely stuck for fear of hurting someone's feelings and they often start sugar-coating the truth. If I honestly thought the Grandma was critical to the arc of the piece, I would have strongly urged Precious to leave it in.

The bottom line? If you're going to write about your life, kill off your internal censor or you'll compromise your honesty, authenticity, and ultimately the spirit of your show. The other option is to create a character who shares many of your characteristics but isn't really you, write your friends and relatives candidly but don't perform in cities where they live.

In the final scene of Seth's show, when Jon-Michael breaks from the seminar's structure and begins to go off track momentarily, we wanted realities to blur. Is it Seth who is freaking out or the character?

Jon-Michael had almost completed the seminar's structure, but it becomes apparent that he's got to go back to an earlier topic and be more truthful.

JON-MICHAEL

The tension was tight at the Tribeca Talent Contest and Cotillion. I tried to stay positive, hoped everybody else would be losers. The real trick is to be nice to people, "Oh, hi, I love your hair." I try to be sincere, but when I can't, I just fake it. I'm wearing the last "I'm Special" T-shirt my mother made for me before she died last September. My heart pounding, I walk onstage. "Tonight, I am going to perform a spoken word presentation of a song that has meant a lot to me. The classic 'Rock the Boat,' by the Hughes Corporation. Ever since our voyage of love began . . . don't rock the boat, baby, rock the . . . boat . . . Rock. The boat." Ramon told me, "How could I pick such an insipid song? Wake up, Jon-Michael, and rock the boat." I'm hearing voices . . . I think it's Melanie. What's she doing in my brain? Beautiful people . . . Stop! Jon-Michael, just stop . . . Stop the boat. Stop the boat!

This was also the show's most autobiographical material, involving his mother's death, which made it significantly more challenging for Seth. Actor and character merged and—even though it's not intended for the audience to necessarily know that—the stakes become higher for both actor and character.

JON-MICHAEL

Okay. Tribeca Talent Contest and Cotillion. Don't be negative; don't be tense. I am a good person and I deserve to win. "Up to now we sailed through every storm . . . Oh, I need to have the strength that flows from you . . ." Shit, I can't remember the last line. Okay, it ends with a word that rhymes with *you*. Boo. Coo. Doo. Foo. Goo. Give me a moment, I'll get it. I have all these people in my brain. It's like they're at the cool people's parties and I'm having a Mary Richards party where nothing ever works out. It's weird. I spent the first half of my life trying to be in. Now I'm spending the second half of my life trying to be out. When I was fourteen, I sat in front of that television set, studying *Love American Style.* I was on my Karen Valentine Attractiveness Training Program. I had pictures of Karen Valentine, Angela Cartwright, and Dawn Wells plastered all over my room. Then I discovered Marlo Thomas. And as hard as I tried, I didn't want to do Marlo Thomas, I wanted to be Marlo Thomas. I wanted Don Hollinger to rescue me. I wanted to be *That Boy.* I was scared. Oh, no. No, homo, don't be a homo. Tell me I didn't say all of this out loud at the Tribeca Talent Contest and Cotillion. I can tell from your silence, I did.

Again, perseverance was key. We rewrote and restaged, then rewrote and restaged it again. And, as often happens, the rest of the show was at the risk of being underrehearsed since this particular scene was being overrehearsed.

On the Wednesday night tech before the Saturday opening, there were the usual challenges to be met: sound cues, missed lines, malfunctioning props, malfunctioning costumes (way before Janet Jackson, I might point out). All of those are pretty much expected but what I hadn't anticipate was the show running an hour and twenty minutes. Oh, my God, I thought to myself, We don't need to cut it, we need to slaughter it.

I get into a lot of arguments on this subject but I'm adamant that a solo show should be performed without an intermission and not much longer than sixty minutes. Unless you're Sir Ian McKellen, and you can mesmerize us for two hours with an intermission, listen to my words. No one is that interesting—especially in this age of fast everything. Even in mainstream theatre, plays are considerably shorter than they used to be, directly attributable to the rise of MTV and the quick cut video.

Seth and I both went home and made our cuts; we disagreed on some, agreed on most, and compromised in several instances. Then he had to memorize the cuts and I had to restage any blocking that was directly affected by the cuts.

I did not go to Vancouver with Precious' show. It would have been too expensive to take me and, besides, my commitment right now was to Seth.

His four previews, one a week, went very well. We rehearsed in between performances, made minor adjustments, and let the material and performance settle. We thought we might make some changes, large or small, before the actual September opening.

Speaking of changes, Precious made an addition to the show in Canada. She told me about it after the fact and it pissed me off. This was my fault because I didn't have a contract that stated "no material can be changed without the approval of the director." Since we'd been working without a contract, I simply assumed that she would honor the fact that my name was on the show as director and material should not be added that I hadn't even seen, let alone directed. In my experience as a writer-performer, I would not introduce material that had not been directed if "directed by Kelly Hill" appeared on the flyer or the program.

Precious created a vagina hand puppet that made an appearance in the final moments of the show, joining Penelope in her closing number. It was, admittedly, very funny. I don't believe for an instant there was any disrespect on her part. She has boundless energy and ingenious ideas, and she acts on them, often independently. She might not even have known about the common etiquette of not changing the show without the director's approval. Change a line or two? Not a problem. But a vagina hand puppet without a director? Could be a problem. As it turned out, it wasn't.

It was one of the occasions when I felt like I deserved to feel disgruntled. And it reminded me that the business in "show business" demands that I have a contractual agreement, no matter how close I am to the artist. A contract is designed to protect the writer-performer as well. What you are giving and what you are expecting to receive needs to be spelled out specifically.

Of her performance in Canada, *Terminal City's* Alan Hindle wrote,

I'm a little lost on this show because the lines are so cleverly
blurred as to whether it's stand-up or performance art. As

stand-up, we're moving into Andy Kauffman territory, where jokes are not necessarily meant to be funny but are expressions of the cracked characters she creates. And they are cracked . . . Occasionally Chong wanders into a fog but then—suddenly! Some laserbeam-sharp observation makes clear she is a performer very much in control of her material.

It was nice to be validated in print.

Noel Alumit, a brilliant writer-performer, saw Seth's final preview and suggested that we build up the mother's role throughout the piece since she is so much a part of the final emotional breakdown. It was a valid point, which Seth and I took to heart. It was the only major change between the final preview and the opening a week later on September 6.

On September 11, 2003, less than a week after Seth's successful opening, Tommy Chong was set to be sentenced. U.S. District Judge Arthur J. Schwab ("like the drugstore," Precious would say in an upcoming show) could sentence Chong to six months to a year in prison, a halfway house, home detention, probation, or some combination of those.

Precious' ability to persevere was made evident but no matter what the outcome of her father's odyssey, she would have to find enormous courage if she planned to continue Porcelain Penelope's odyssey.

Exercise/Perseverance

If you're human, at this point you've probably grown weary of these exercises. And you probably feel like stopping or jumping ahead to the last one. Or just throwing out those silly exercises, convincing yourself it wasn't any good anyway. In fact, it's probably even crossed your mind to stop reading this wacky book because you'll never get it together to do a solo show in this lifetime.

Now is the time to persevere. Summon the drive to move forward. Pray. Call a friend. Go see a one-person show or rent one at the video store. Do whatever it takes to keep moving ahead with the project.

Ready? Committed? Put self-doubt and self-criticism on hold and get back to some writing.

This time I want you to write about two separate incidents—both of them related to the defining event that happened to you in kindergarten. One should be a fairly positive experience and the other should be a not-so-positive experience. And these events should have occurred in your adulthood.

Let me provide an example. In kindergarten, remember those artsy things you made with an indentation of your handprint that were designed to hang on the wall? Ours were green with a red ribbon—maybe they were Christmas presents? Anyway, mine broke before I got it home and the teacher said, rather dramatically, "Mike's hand is broken" and almost all my peers thought I had literally broken my hand. I was mortified. Later, as an acting student, my hands were my nemesis and I think it had to do with feeling like I'd give away my gayness if I did the wrong thing (too flighty, too dramatic) on- or offstage with my hands. So I was somewhat paralyzed. Not good. After I came out and started doing solo work, my hands were almost always mentioned in reviews as being one of the most expressive parts of my body. It's as if I had held back all those years and I finally liberated the expression in my hands. A good thing.

Spend no more than an hour total on both of these. Again, don't get too heady. Don't try to impose a theme or a story or a happy ending. Just write.

When you finish, the reward for your perseverance will be that you probably have several pages of rough narrative.

Chapter 4 Checklist

- When faced with a challenge, are you a quitter or a person who perseveres?

- Perseverance is required in order to embrace the process. Are you more concerned with the result?

- Are you willing to persevere even though your work may not be perfect at every stage?

- Can you persevere even when your expectations aren't met?
- Are you flexible in a crisis, especially one that potentially affects your show?
- Can you take criticism, even if it's unfair?
- Do you have the discipline to rehearse by yourself?
- Are you willing to cut material if it doesn't serve the story even if that material shows you in your best light?
- If writing autobiographically, have you considered the stakes in revealing personal history?
- Are you able (and willing) to tell your story in approximately an hour?

5 Courage

Fear is not enough to stop the human spirit.

Dan Kwong

PRECIOUS

It won't take me but a second to set up. I was stuck on the 5, coming from Taft Prison in Kern Country. I'm Precious Chong, Tommy Chong's daughter. I just came from visiting him in the slammer. He was sentenced to nine months. Tommy Chong of Cheech & Chong. The other one. The one who was not on *Nash Bridges*. My dad got busted by the Feds. Operation Pipe Dreams. Another case of life imitating art. Badly.

These lines opened our return to the Masquers on October 16, eight days after Tommy went to jail (the first of only three performances she would do of this version). She entered through the audience wearing a red-, white-, and blue-spangled bikini with a matching beret.

I hoped that the costume would set the tone for this installment of what was becoming a series of Porcelain Penelope shows, the (newly titled) *Porcelain Penelope Goes to Washington* show. You don't want to be funny for the sake of being funny nor do you want to be political for the sake of being political. But I wanted to let the audience know that we are going to tell a story that is both funny and political.

The costume also let them know that we're going to tease the truth. While it was a fact that her dad was in the slammer, we know that she didn't really visit him in that get-up. I also felt that the sexiness of the costume—a red-, white-, and blue-glittering tribute to the American flag—made a statement about freedom of expression that, along with

71

all civil rights, are being threatened by the administration that put her dad in jail. The audience howled with laughter. For Precious, it wasn't entirely a laughing matter.

While Precious and I had certainly formed a friendship, we rarely hung out with each other in between gigs. We'd exchanged a few phone messages, but I didn't really know what she'd been going through until I read the new pages.

Her writing had changed dramatically, fueled by anger, fear, embarrassment, and, perhaps most important, love. If we thought she had something to write about before this tumultuous event, consider what she had to put on paper now. And when I say *had to,* I mean had to. It saved her in ways that I don't believe either of us could completely articulate. She had a source to channel her growing frustration and rage.

"This is the hardest thing you'll ever do," Alec Mapa says, "but trust that the best thing that could possibly ever happen is what usually happens. I can only see this in hindsight, because I've written three solo comedies and they're all about shitty things that happened to me and the lessons learned therein. The story of obstacles overcome is everyone's story. The more specific you are, the more universal you become."

Precious also had courage. Even my then nine-year-old daughter, who didn't see the show but was aware of the content, said, "She's brave not to care if people will make fun of her." I explained to Tia that Precious had enormous courage. "Like the lion," she answered. "Exactly," I said.

My job was to make sure, as complicated at the text had become, that Precious always maintained a level of entertainment. And to not let her lose her fabulous sense of humor. We walked a very fine line.

PRECIOUS

I feel like Nancy Drew. A sleuth. Uncovering the clues that led to my father being fucked by the federal government. Screwed up the ass by Ashcroft. Buggered by Mary Beth Buchanan. It makes me want to make a porno. A bad porno. Where I wear this outfit and get it good from a huge black man with the biggest cock you've ever seen in your life. Then I'm going to

72

smoke pot. Take a bong hit and then drink the water. Bathe in
it. Wash my hair in it so I smell like skunk, like Acapulco Gold.
Like the strongest BC Bud that ever existed. I'm going to do all
this while I listen to Eminem and watch Howard Stern while I'm
thumbing through Hustler. Then I'm going to buy all of the Girls
Gone Wild videos—Spring Break, Mexico, etcetera. Then I'm
going to do performance art. In Pittsburgh. I'm going to take a
big poop in front of the courthouse while two gay men get married by a dyke priest. After that I'll go and get an abortion or
two. Then I think I'll feel better. I think.

This was staged with her striking a series of nasty poses accompanied by a percussive underlay from our new onstage musician, Gilbran
Chong (Precious' brother). Even though this monologue was highly
entertaining, it came from a place of utter rage. Notice that she was no
longer camouflaging her identity; this was Precious Chong speaking,
even though it was an obvious fantasy.

It doesn't take Dr. Phil to tell you that rage is usually ignited by
love. It was the love of her father that put her in this state of anger,
which played as a kind of theatrical dementia. Again, this isn't anger for
anger's sake and it is not out of control. She is telling a story, not simply being angry.

In addition to the anger that was now in the writing, there were
some lovely passages, serving as memories of her dad.

PRECIOUS

When I had chicken pox, my dad took the swing from outside
and put it up in the doorway in the hall outside my room so
that I could swing on that swing but basically stay inside. I was
three years old.

Perhaps the only thing worse than seeing someone spew anger
onstage is listening to gooey sentimentality. What I've said about funny,
political, and angry also applies to lovely writing. We always had to
know when to stop or switch gears, never letting things get too over-
heated or too maudlin or go on too long.

In that respect, solo acting is no different than any other kind of acting. You don't play a result (angry, happy, sad, hurt, silly). You play an intention.

The intention of the soloist, first and foremost, is to tell a story. Within that framework, there are dozens upon dozens of actable intentions: to contradict, to defend, to challenge, to seduce, to hurt, to justify, to tease, to inspire, and on and on. Every word and physical action has an intention that feeds the primary intention: I want to tell you a story. The only way to state it more strongly would be, I must tell you a story.

There were several new threads in *Porcelain Penelope Goes to Washington*. One of them was a series of conversations with Dr. Sheila Balkan, the criminologist who was on Chong's side. In reality, this consisted of one phone call but for the purposes of the show, we stretched it out into several in-person meetings. The material Precious had written was just too outrageous.

PRECIOUS

(*To Sheila*) Look, even though I grew up in what you consider a freak show, I'm together. I'm normal. I'm just like you. (*To audience*) But I'm not. She wears clothes from Anne Taylor. She was probably in a sorority. She's so cautious I want to shake her. (*As Sheila*) Tell me, Precious—is that your real name?—what was it like growing up with Tommy Chong as a father?

These Sheila reenactments, if you will, were played in the playing area—onstage, if you will—where the numbers took place, separate from what happened backstage. Her backstage monologues were more intimately delivered directly to the audience.

At one point in her conversations with Sheila, in an attempt to seem normal, Precious points out that she studied ballet and Shakespeare. Hmmm, I thought to myself, there's a direction for the director to take. She had also described her family's various responses to her dad being locked up as "Shakespearean."

"Read *King Lear*," I suggested, "and see if there's something you can pull that mirrors how you're feeling." This was a way to be very emotional but using the Bard's words, not hers. The next day at rehearsal, she came in with several lines that Cordelia delivers to her father and we began sprinkling them throughout the show.

Not only did the Shakespeare provide her a way to express extreme emotion that might have veered toward gushing had we used her words, the sudden outbursts created a heightened sense of her precarious emotional state. Even before adding her father's happenings to the show, there was an underlying sense of the characters taking over (especially, for instance, Mr. H and the Talking Vagina); she wasn't always in control of them. We used this with Shakepeare as well—it was as if she went into another stratosphere and words came pouring out.

PRECIOUS

(As Cordelia)
What shall Cordelia speak?
Love and be silent?

As for performing the ballet, well, consider the space limitations. I'd asked a lot of Kim but this verged on being a ridiculous request. But Kim managed to create a ballet to words. The delicacy of the movement was, of course, intended to offset the tough reality of the confessional.

PRECIOUS

The mythology of my childhood. I was conceived on acid. My dad was a comedian. My name was Precious. How do you spell that? A comedian. In kindergarten, "What's a comedian?" Once two fans came backstage after one of their shows and one of them had jeans on and they were soaked. "Man, I laughed so hard, I peed my pants." Even at the age of six or seven, I thought, "Oh, brother." My Dad and Cheech laughed. What was he like as a father? What's it like to have Chong as a dad? Do you guys get stoned? I bet he has the best bud. Maybe it was different for my brothers. I was straight. I was boring. Shakespeare. I was a ballerina. I wanted to go to ballet school in Russia. I wanted to go to school in the USSR. I thought LA was full of it. Not real, not real. Now communism? That's real.

"We talked about this yearning she had for discipline," Kim said. "Precious wanted real ballet training, not peeing in one's pants stories. It was a contrast of what is thought of as elevated culture set against the counterculture. It was her trying to be proper and pretty in an irreverent world."

Again, it was about the odd juxtaposition of the words and the ballet—something we kept in mind for the future.

Making another choice, instead of contrasting, we matched the music with the text; in fact, we broke one of my cardinal rules about not using familiar song lyrics. In this case, as Precious delivered yet another response to Sheila, it cried out for the Stones. Instead of ballet, she just danced demonically.

PRECIOUS

Once when we were driving back from a screening of Cheech & Chong's *Nice Dreams,* I was sitting in the back, leaning forward between him and my mom and said, "You're gonna win an Oscar." The movie was that good. That funny. Cheech crawling up the glass elevator while the Stones sang, "I Can't Get No Satisfaction." What's it like to have Chong as a dad? "Well, Sheila, we get stoned all the time. Our house is sort of like *Charlie and the Chocolate Factory* except instead of candy, it's marijuana. And hallucinogens. Acid and peyote and mushrooms and hashish. At Thanksgiving we have a turkey like everyone else, but ours is stuffed with bud. Then we really are hungry after all the marijuana. Then we laugh and laugh and mom rings out a huge heaping pile of brownies. Yum. Then we pass the bong around while we watch the *South Park* marathon. We're just your typical happy all-American family."

Talk about effective use of hyperbole. And her delivery mixed wackiness with an edge of danger. Precious was never getting off; she was always performing while playing an intention. There's a difference. She obviously had a point to make and we found a way to do it so that it was outlandishly funny but, because she's a trained actress, also angry.

Tommy Chong's charges had been blown out of proportion and that's what his daughter was doing with her fantasy response to Sheila—blowing it out of proportion.

Another significant change was with the Sexy Mom material. She, too, was experiencing life-changing episodes that Precious chose not to ignore.

Sexy Mom

They raided our house, Precious. Those DNA—I mean D-E-A people—they raided our house. Helicopters, swat teams. It's ridiculous. We don't even lock our door. They've taken everything. They just left. They took the glass pipes but left the plastic ones. I told them, I told those cops they better move those cars before they scare Myra off. Who's Myra? Our new maid. And they wouldn't let Dad go down to Starbucks to get our cappuccinos. I told them that "there is a princess on board." Well, that made the dyke lady cop laugh. They told Dad if he pleads guilty they won't charge Paris or me. He'll get a fine and house arrest. Can you imagine house arrest? That's punishment for the wife. They also found Dad's stash from the fans. A pound. Precious, it's not that much. A pound of coffee, a pound of flour. Honey, I can't talk on this phone; it's probably being tapped. I gotta go. I don't want to be late for my hip-hop class. Frank's teaching a new combination.

This change in Mom's voice is significant because Precious maintains the comedic aspect of the character but, because her mother was becoming a bit less frivolous in real life, she allowed the character to begin what would be a significant change of values and perspective.

Tahmus left the show because of other commitments and we let Amy out of her thankless role as his mute girlfriend and the overworked dresser of Precious/Penelope. We were back to a one-person show—well, almost. There was that brother/drummer (who did two out of three at this venue), replaced by Clinton Cameron for the final performance of this round. Clinton played the drums with a sense of fierce theatricality.

Because of time considerations, the Hooligan was let go. In the scheme of things, what he represented was less important than what the other characters and the new material brought to *Porcelain Penelope Goes to Washington.*

The Hooligan represented, along with Mr. H, the maleness that is a part of Precious. While Mr. H is strict and hurtful and unforgiving, the Hooligan is a hedonist who was crude, horny, and lascivious. The audience loved him and his monologue did provide a clean break in the progression of the show. But was he necessary? No, and he really wasn't missed.

Mr. H, however, ran the show (from inside Precious' head) so he remained with updated commentary to deal with the new material.

MR. H

Ms. Chong, I would appreciate it if you would please stop bab-
bling and put on your costume. Do you want to get your father
in more trouble? It's called a gag order for a reason.

In truth, there was no gag order and now that her dad was incar-
cerated, there was no fear of any recriminations. It's one of the many things that freed her.

We worked quickly, as usual; since we knew the space, the tech was less stressful. And the show was beginning to—dare I say it?—calm down. It might not sound like it but amidst the new high-pitched material, most of which was delivered to the imaginary Sheila, there were plenty of very soft moments that led to a conclusion that I felt had the potential to be breathtaking.

As with the first ending at the Masquers, we played with the idea that Precious had rid herself of her alter egos. After the show ended, she got a microphone and decided to work on some stand-up material. Somewhere along the line, and this realization was more dramatically justified with the real-life incidents being part of the script, she had to let go of all pretense and allow herself to be Precious. Alone. At the mike.

This is where the universality of her show becomes apparent. Perhaps we all engage in playing a variety of roles before we arrive at our authentic self. And we often overplay a role and become self-destructive in the process. Precious/Penelope knows this too well when she says, "Pretty soon I won't be able to do this little girl act anymore."

While not always considered actors, good stand-ups deliver from a place of authenticity. It is why many of them adapt to acting so naturally. The acceptance of self (even if it's distorted) is the badge of most stand-ups. They have taken a shortcut. In many instances, actors play many roles in order to arrive at a true self. With stand-ups, it's the acceptance of self that allows them to play many roles.

Standing at the mike also pointed to the notion that Precious was carrying on a family tradition, a fact that made her dad proud. And ironically, even though we didn't say it out loud, she was also emerging from her father's shadow. The fact that he was in the pokey, I speculated, had something to do with her leap into new territory as an artist and a human being. She could no longer rely on his presence—physical, at least—to complete her identity. A bittersweet reality.

She tried to remain neutral. Obviously, any sadness that her father experienced was painful for her, but she was proud of herself for accepting the changes that were happening to her. Remember when I said there's a point at which you allow things to happen? We couldn't have imposed this on the show a year prior—it would have been false. But Precious had the courage to take what was happening in her life and put it on the stage without a trace of self-indulgence. It was a remarkable feat.

We were ready to open.

In the October 16 issue of *Daily Variety*, the venerable Army Archerd wrote:

> Tommy Chong's daughter Precious performs her (very political) one-woman piece, *Porcelain Penelope Goes to Washington* at the Masquers Cabaret tonight and October 23 and hopes to visit her father this weekend in the Taft minimum security prison near Bakersfield. She and her mom Shelby are hoping to organize a benefit to try and change the current law that put Tommy in jail for nine months.

Like a train chugging forward to its destination, you must stay on track. If the train is going from Los Angeles to Phoenix, it must stop at certain stations along the way as it gets closer and closer to its destination. Think of your show's speeches or character's confessions or monologues as stations on the path to a destination.

I'm not necessarily looking for a resolved ending; life is messy, and solo shows can be as well. But they need a punctuation mark at the end—a period or an exclamation point. Maybe even a question mark if it comes as a result of a journey. Let the audience know that, at least for now, you've arrived at your destination.

Let's review the endings of the many versions of *The Porcelain Penelope Show*. The first workshop production virtually ended with Grandma's monologue followed by a short Penelope bit and a vague windup where Precious' words and actions indicated that, with the help of the snake book, she had learned something about herself. We didn't really earn that ending; it wasn't organic. We made it happen.

In our first Zephyr show, we created an intricate finale that may have been a bit ambitious and somewhat convoluted. When we moved to the Masquers, we cut the piece and restaged it so it was more intimate and less busy in terms of physicality. It definitely changed the tone and was much easier for the audience to grasp. Along with the political stakes, the emotional stakes were considerably higher in this new version—especially the ending.

After Tommy's arrest and incarceration, there were brand-new endings, sometimes occurring within days of being re-created on the stage. We always had to consider the entire show—every section, every page, every word—needed to point in the direction of the ending. If it didn't, it had to be rewritten or cut. What was interesting is that material written more than a year before fed the "real-life" ending.

In many ways, you can work backward. Think of your show as a train excursion. Check the route you've taken to make certain you have stayed on track, not missed any significant stops along the way, or made any unnecessary stops. Also, like a train, you have a schedule. The train leaves at a certain time and arrives at its destination at a certain time (within five or ten minutes).

Precious is not one of those actresses who turn on tears like a faucet in order to impress us with her crying abilities (I don't have a clue where it was written that if you can cry on cue, you can act. It's bullshit.) Precious would often cry when reading something for the first time and I'd say, "Remember that. Don't forget the purity of that moment." I wasn't asking her to cry again. I was asking her to relive the authenticity of what she had experienced as a result of saying the words out loud for the first time.

All performance should feel like the words are being said for the first time. In the Grandma speech, for instance, there was a moment when the character recounts the death of her son. Precious broke down the first few times she did it but then she, as the character and as herself, became determined not to cry. This was the appropriate intention, if you will, of the Grandma. She did not want to be perceived as a crybaby (and neither did the actress, for that matter).

Imagine an actress delivering the speech below in tears. Then imagine an actress fighting the tears. Which would be more effective?

GRANDMA

My son. My first child. He was hit in the temple. He was hit in the temple with a baseball bat. He came home and we put him to bed. We put him to bed. He was hit in the temple. My son. I knew, I always did. I always do. When something bad had happened. I have that gift. All the women in my family have it. I just knew it. I told him, I told Harry, "We should take him to the hospital." But he wouldn't listen to me, he wouldn't listen. He just told me I worry too much. I worry. I do. But we just called that darn doctor of his, one of Harry's drinking buddies, who told us to give him an aspirin and send him to bed. Well, later that night, Murray cried out. He cried out, he cried out in the middle of the night. And, well, Harry just yelled at him to go back to sleep. In the morning, in the morning, he was gone. We don't talk about it. My boy. My boy, Murray. So handsome, such a beautiful handsome boy. But don't talk about it. Put it away put it away for later. I'm putting it away for later.

It's like playing a drunk—a lesson that I repeat to my acting students on a regular basis. To play a drunk realistically, the intention is to act like you're not drunk.

The monologue that would precede the new ending at the Masquers in the fall of her dad's sentence was critical preparation for the emotional climax that would follow it. Not only was it a potentially sad moment, it was about crying, which made it even more complex to act and direct.

PRECIOUS

The day my father is sentenced to federal prison, I have a commercial audition for Ace Hardware at the funky Ferrets. Keep it small, keep it real, keep it ferret. The spot is of a couple having an anniversary dinner and the husband hands his wife an awful-looking gift wrapped in newspaper. She is supposed to start to cry—the viewer thinks it because of the awful gift but then she says, reading an ad on the newspaper gift-wrapping, "I'm the luckiest woman in the world. Ace Hardware is having a sale!" The casting director says, "Precious, it would be great if there were real tears." I try it once. "I'm the luckiest woman in the world. Ace Hardware is having a sale!" No tears. I try it again. "I'm the luckiest woman in the world. Ace Hardware is having a sale!" Again, dry as a bone. "I'm sorry," I say to the casting director, "I'm having trouble with my emotions." And then I started to cry. And he starts to film me. *(Almost sobbing)* "I'm the luckiest woman in the world. Ace Hardware is having a sale!" I see him sort of laugh at me. Nervously. But then it's over and I still can't stop. I cannot stop crying at a commercial audition. Everyone is bewildered. They don't know what to do with me. "I'm sorry," I say, and I leave.

It was tricky. You can imagine what Lucy Ricardo would do with it. You can also imagine what Sissy Spacek would do with it. I certainly wanted the heartbreak, but I also wanted the humor. Did I want tears? It had to feed the ending of the show, not rob it.

It was almost as if the commercial speech was the preparation for the ending which, essentially, happened on the same day (in real life). The new ending was performed at the mike, with a follow spot on her face. A bit stark.

<small>PRECIOUS</small>

(*Precious*) Later that night I finally talk to my dad. He calls my cell phone. (*Shakespeare*) "Come, let's away to prison. We to alone will sing like birds in the cage." (*Precious*) His voice sounds tired, relieved but he speaks to me in an urgent way. (*Shakespeare*) "When thou dost ask me blessing, I'll kneel down, and ask of thee forgiveness." (*Tommy*) Precious, I can't do my show. (*Shakespeare*) "So we'll live and pray, and sing, and tell old tales, and laugh at gilded butterflies." (*Tommy*) They're not going to let me do stand-up anymore. (*Shakespeare*) ". . .and hear poor rogues talk of court news" (*Tommy*) Precious, they talked about *Up in Smoke*. They said I spoke to the press with a smirk on my face. (*Shakespeare*) ". . . and we'll talk with them too—who loses and who wins, who's in, who's out . . ." (*Newscaster*) "The defendant has become wealthy throughout his entertainment career by glamorizing the illegal distribution and use of marijuana." (*Shakespeare*) "And take upon's the mystery of things as if we were God's spies." (*Mary McKeen Houghton, Assistant to the U.S. Attorney*) "Feature films that he made with his longtime partner, Cheech Marin, such as *Up in Smoke*, trivialize law enforcement efforts to combat marijuana trafficking and use." (*Precious*) I'm so sorry, Dad. (*Tommy*) It's up to you, now, Precious, you have to keep performing. Keep writing. You have to be my voice. (*Shakespeare*) "And we'll wear out in a walled prison pacts and sects of great ones that ebb and flow by the moon." (*Precious*) No, Dad, I have to be my voice. Just like you, Dad. Just like you.

Precious performed it quite simply, only hinting at duplicating the sound of her dad's voice and the newscaster's voice. Trust equals simplicity.

It was quite an ending. Again, not necessarily a happy ending. Dad's in jail. She's not consistently being the dutiful daughter. But, on some level, in the way only a solo show can reveal in sixty minutes— she has discovered her own voice. And it's not Penelope's or Snake Girl's or Mom's or Emma's or Mr. H's or the Talking Vagina's. It's her voice— found at last.

On the first night, Jenny brought Precious' "sisters" from *Lughnasa* (Bonnie Franklin, Susan Clark, and Stephanie Zimbalist), who very much played the supportive and proud role of big sisters. Jenny suggested that we put Mr. H on tape. I'm not sure why I resisted but I did. Maybe I was being stubborn or maybe I wanted to "showcase" the many voices of Precious Chong—neither justified keeping the voice live. But we did.

On the third and final night, we got Steve Mikulin, a very respected writer from the *LA Weekly* to see the show, which resulted in a very well-written and positive article. She performed this show only three times to overwhelming positive response. "Real courage," David Nichols says, "is unaware of itself, but to those who witness it in action, it is unmistakable and unforgettable."

We were done. There was no audience demand to keep the show open and I think she accomplished what she had set out to do. Or had she? And if not, would she possibly be able to find the stamina to revise Porcelain Penelope's adventures one more time? Maybe this was the "happy ending" after all.

Exercise/Courage

I often ask my acting students (even if they are doing a scene that would be considered light comedy), "What scares you about doing this scene?" If they look at me like I'm crazy and say, "Nothing," I immediately shoot back, "Then find something."

When I say "scares," I don't mean like a horror movie. I'm asking what makes you nervous or apprehensive or possibly embarrassed? In other words, what gets your motor running? What about the material makes your heart beat? What about the material makes you a bit queasy? Where's the danger? What are the stakes?

This takes courage. Look over the three sections you've written. (This is also a point at which you might decide to make this a fictitious story as opposed to autobiography—that's fair.) And apply some of these questions to your work. What do you risk when you present this material to an audience? This is a thought process and probably can't be done in a specified amount of time. Let it gestate for a few days.

These feelings are subjective, by the way. It doesn't have to be a story about killing your neighbor's cat. It could be something that makes you feel stupid, or silly, or immature, or not very sophisticated. But you need to find something that compels you to tell the story, something that requires a bit of courage.

Chapter 5 Checklist

- As a writer, can you communicate the courage of your convictions?

- Do you have the courage to be unpopular?

- Do you have the courage to fail along the way?

- Do you have the courage to take chances, physically and vocally, as a performer?

- Do you have the courage to go deeper even when it's painful?

- Do you have the courage to face an audience that may not be on your side?

- If your work has an angry edge, are you able to find interesting ways to express it?

- Can you personalize autobiographical elements without being self-indulgent?

6 Stamina

Solo performance demands the stamina and [the] stick-to-it-ivness of a pit bull running a marathon to turn in a winning lottery ticket!

Tim Miller

She had never looked so radiantly beautiful. We had established our favorite lunch ritual and inevitably one of us was running late. On this picture-perfect California May day, I happened to be a bit early and sat in the café facing a window with the Beverly Boulevard in clear view.

Suddenly, there she was, ignoring the crosswalks and defying the cars, moving toward the trendy café where I was waiting. Her hair was longer and she had on a skimpy black dress with oversized black sunglasses. She had on a big lime-green straw hat and was carrying a bag with what looked like typewritten pages sticking out of it, possibly about to blow away.

Precious Chong looked like a movie star—confident, sexy, and self-possessed.

More than six months had elapsed. We'd run into each other maybe a couple of times but our exchanges were usually brief bits of Hollywood chitchat. This was going to be a real meeting with an agenda.

"You look fabulous, honey," I said, as we hugged. In that moment, I realized how much I had missed her. We each had news to share and after the fun exchange of gossip, we ordered lunch and got down to business.

She had managed the nearly impossible. After making an in-person visit and dropping off a tape at The Culture Project at 45 Bleecker, she got a booking. This is not the usual route by which a West Coast solo show makes it to New York. It was a matter of the timing and a combination of her in-person sales ability and the quality of the show. She was asked by Alan Buchman to be part of the Women Center Stage 2004 Festival.

My news was equally exciting. I'd been contracted to write a solo book and, with her permission, I would make *The Porcelain Penelope Show* the primary example of one solo journey. She was delighted.

Because of what had been going on in her personal life since our last performance in the fall of 2003, the show needed a complete overhaul.

We were also both determined to make the New York installment the very best *Porcelain Penelope Show* ever. We anticipated that the rewrite would be extensive enough to require a series of workshop performances. Since the playing area in New York would more closely resemble the Zephyr, we got in touch with Gary and Linda. They welcomed us back for four consecutive Tuesday nights in June. During our lunch meeting, Precious gave me a copy of the most recent script and several additional new pages.

By this point in our collaboration, we had developed a game plan that worked. I would study the new pages and make suggestions as to how I felt they would best be incorporated. That also meant identifying an equivalent number of cuts. We would have a script meeting several days before the first day of a tight rehearsal schedule. We would begin with a brand-new draft, subject to changes based on putting the material up on its feet.

We began one week prior to the first Tuesday workshop. Not only did we have to stage the additions, we had to reblock and refresh some of the old material because it had been months since the most recent performance at the Masquers.

The bulk of the new work centered on Precious visiting her dad in prison. Other changes included a more political Mom, a few minor changes to "I've Written a Letter . . . ," and a number of New York laugh lines (we hoped) for Mr. H. There was also a new opening, a new closing, and a new light plot to work out with Gary.

We had to remind ourselves that this was a month of workshops with a week in between to rewrite, reconsider, and restage. We didn't have to accomplish everything by the time Tuesday arrived.

Just as we finished lunch and paid the bill (my turn), she announced, "I'm engaged."

"You're what?" I said, wondering if I misheard her.

"I'm engaged. To an actor I met in Canada."

"Was he in the show you did?" I asked. She had just returned from doing a play in Canada in which she played a female werewolf.

"Yes," she said with a mischievous grin. "He proposed to me on opening night, which happened to be my birthday. And then he proposed every night of the run."

"Name?"

"Wes," she said, as we gathered our stuff and headed out on to the busy street. Now we were both in the middle of the traffic with some cars slowing down and others ignoring us. I just couldn't keep myself from pursuing the engagement, knowing it would have to be part of the show.

"Is it significant in any way that you got engaged while your dad is in prison?" I asked. We'd made it to the opposite side of the street. Her face went blank but only for a split second.

"I didn't think of that," she said.

"It's my job," I reminded her. "It has to go in the show. The engagement will be the new ending, won't it?" It wasn't really a question. We hugged again and set the time for our first meeting to explore the text.

In between *Porcelain Penelope Goes to Washington* and what would be retitled *The Porcelain Penelope Freak Show*, the world of solo performance lost one of its greatest monologists, Spalding Gray. Ruthlessly blurring the line between art and reality, Gray disappeared on January 10, 2004. Just prior to his disappearance, he had taken his two young sons, Theo and Forrest, to see the Tim Burton film *Big Fish*, a movie in which an adult son struggles to understand and know his father, a perennial spinner of tales.

That same night, after dropping the boys off at home, he made a phone call to his sons to say good night. Police traced the call to a pay phone at the Staten Island Ferry. Even his final moments had a sense of theatricality about them, almost as if he lived life in order to write it.

But he could no longer write. A disabling automobile accident a few years before had resulted in a brain injury. In an interview with Liz Weisstuch of the *Harvard Gazette* in January 2002, he said, "It's hard for me to speak because I'm in a state of despair now. I think the monologue is always seeking to at least express the balance in a story, if not in real life. It usually reflects falling apart and coming together again." Unable to use the monologue to save his life, there would be no "coming together again." His badly decomposed body was recovered from the East River in March 2004.

"He was the first actor I knew who was working with his persona as a meta-persona," said Kate Valk, a Wooster Group member. Perhaps the proximity of his death made the parallels to Precious' exploration of her persona even more artistically exciting and dangerous. My respect for her and everyone who does this rigorous work increased with the loss of Gray.

I e-mailed Precious with some notes before our meeting on June 1. The bulk of the new material takes place inside the prison walls and her writing had become even richer, funnier, sadder, and tougher. I made some cuts, cleaned up some things that were confusing, and suggested an order that punched up the evolving theme.

At the conclusion of *Porcelain Penelope Goes to Washington,* she had found her voice. Now she had found a husband. What she had initially told me when we sat in my living room two years before was that her show was about a daughter escaping from the shadow cast by her famous (and now infamous) father. What was so compelling to me about this two-year process is how life informed her art and art informed her life. It truly became so entwined that it became impossible for me (and I honestly think, at times, for her) to tell the difference.

Subtler but no less exciting, the new script embraced her role as an outsider, a rebel, and a freak. Yes, *The Porcelain Penelope Freak Show* became our new title. When I first suggested it, I wasn't sure she'd go for it but she did. The title itself became a bold statement. A freak show is, by definition, a sideshow featuring freaks of nature. A *freak* could be defined as someone who is unusual or abnormal. A sexual deviant is also known as a freak. To some degree, they all apply to the cast of characters in the show.

I relate to the word in the same way that I relate to *queer*. Self-describing oneself as a *queer* or a *freak* is an assertive act, owning a word that has been a negative and making it a positive.

We met for our first rehearsal. At this point, we could actually block, rewrite, and reconstruct things simultaneously. And that's what we did. We worked for a few hours a day doing just that, knowing that we would bring in Clinton, the drummer, at the end of the week and be ready for a tech rehearsal with Gary on Sunday.

The new opening we created let the audience know that the importance of a mainstream career has taken a back seat to what she's doing in the moment: performing live. Is she pissed off? Yep, but she makes us laugh and invites us in immediately.

PRECIOUS

So I'm sitting on the plane, eating my snack, and watching those little TVs, and *Friends* comes on—my episode, sort of. You see, my best friend used to date one of the executive producers on the show and in the historic first episode of the last season he writes a character named Precious. Character breakdown—"Precious: female attractive late 20s, early 30s, must be good with comedy." I do not get to even audition for the role. I'm not the right type. I remember when he asked me if it was okay if he used my name in the show. "Sure," I said, thinking that it was just going to be referred to and not actually be a real live character on *Friends*. Not that an actual actress would be playing the role and that actress would not be me. That I wouldn't be right for the role of myself. So there I am, watching it and I see the girl. The girl playing me. She's blonde, tall, round-faced, pretty, sweet-looking. Younger. Precious. You know what, Andrew? You can kiss my precious ass!

Note how she delivers a very strong statement without ever spelling out her cause. By the time she finishes this speech we know that she is righteously pissed off at Hollywood's abuse of actors (especially women) but she doesn't make an announcement. Tell a story to make your point rather than stating it like a newspaper editorial.

We cut several of the Sheila scenes, but not all of them since they established so much of the bond between Precious and her dad. But the scenes that would give the new show its emotional wallop were the scenes that actually occur between Tommy and Precious in jail.

We had the advantage of knowing the ending—the destination of the train ride. So what we had to do was create the various stops along the way. Since the final scene would show Precious telling her dad that she's going to get married and how he reacts—why not begin the show there by teasing the ending and then essentially presenting everything else as flashbacks?

PRECIOUS

It's just me and my dad on this last visit, May 28, 2004. It's nice to have him all to myself. Dad, I've got something to tell you.

We had yet to discover how that key line ("Dad, I've got something to tell you"), repeated nearly an hour later, would remind the audience that we were picking up where we left off during the final visit. But trust me, we would nail it.

In addition to the scenes in the prison visiting room, there were scenes in the car with Precious and Shelby, her mom, on their way to the prison and then on their return. In these scenes, Precious moved from the passenger seat to the driver's seat, as deftly as she changed from playing her mom to playing herself. Like the Sheila scenes, where she often stepped out of her role in order to share an intimate memory with the audience, the scenes depicting the prison visits also led to some sweet reveries.

PRECIOUS

When I was really little, I remember when Dad and Cheech were on the road for the first time. My mom and Cheech's girl-friend at the time, a redhead with big boobs, Barbie, who made me a birthday cake with jellybeans on it, were supposed to pick them up at LAX. The day was spent in preparation. I remember the warm fresh smell of my mom blow-drying her hair and putting on her cute mini-dress. Then we all loaded into the tiny MG Convertible to drive to the airport. We got lost on the free-way. I remember the yellow lights of a deserted street as my mom and Barbie looked at a map. My mom was only 23. We were two hours late picking them up. Dad and Cheech waited.

Placement of the new scenes (not only on the page but on the stage), in addition to the established scenes, became critical in terms of the show's emotional flow, not forgetting the practical aspects of lighting those areas and being aware of sight lines. We established the locations: the dressing room upstage; the playing area downstage, which encom-passed the Sheila office (stage right); the car (center stage); the prison area (primarily stage left but utilizing the entire stage at some points); and the intimate areas (located literally in the aisles of the audience).

We also had to consider the style of each scene and how to make the various styles coalesce. In addition to the gallery of show-biz char-acters who were drawn to the spotlight, we now had prison scenes that I wanted to be played with a certain stark reality.

PRECIOUS

Inside we get BBQ chicken wings—two packs for $6 and microwave popcorn. I lose the first $6 because I panic and slide open an empty chute. Then I have to fill out a form and wait for the concession man to come. A ruddy-faced white guy with a huge gut. Makes some comment about my name. He fills up the machine real slow. Punishing. Visitors: big women in tight jeans, a Latin father with a cranky face, a thin blonde woman, her face pinched by nerves. Inside the visiting area, we sit on those hard chairs and talk. Dad tells us about his life inside. There's Big Ben, a huge Samoan who protects my dad and comes to sit with us. His arms are the size of tree trunks and he speaks in a weird Chicano/Hawaiian mumble. There are three TV rooms and one has on sports 24/7. There's a movie every Saturday night. This week's movie? *The Hours.*

Shifting acting modes turned out to be our biggest challenge. Precious had perfected moving from one character to another, but moving from style to style was a bit more challenging. This is an effective aspect of solo performance but probably explored less because it requires a performer with chops. And stamina.

The direction of a piece—from the page to the stage—will be influenced by how well you can act. As a director, I must respect an actor's limitations. Training is key—everything from acting classes to fencing classes, from vocal techniques to movement techniques. The performer with a trained instrument will be better able to bring a solo piece to life, physically and vocally, than will someone who is not trained.

This does not mean that you need a degree from Juilliard to do a solo piece. It does mean that the untrained performer will likely be restricted in areas of physical and vocal expression. If this is the case, I suggest that the piece's literary value may still be considerable. While it is ideal to have strengths in both disciplines to make solo work shine, strength in one can—to a degree—compensate for weakness in the other.

Someone with a strong writing technique and a strong desire to perform their own material should seek the opinion of a truthful theatre director or acting teacher. Remember, there's the option of hiring an actor to do your show. Considering the emotional range that's required, you may not be the best person to serve your own material.

There are exceptions. Consider the natural-born entertainer who has little or no training but seems to belong on a stage. Or the natural-born storyteller whose writing seems to flow fluidly. But no matter how gifted the aspiring soloist may be, training will serve to enhance your gifts.

Assess your strengths and weaknesses. An actor who has never written could benefit from a writing class and a writer who has never performed should check into some acting classes. "You will be supported and bolstered by the depth and level of your own abilities as a writer and performer," Mark Travis points out. "You can show your best, avoid your weaknesses. But," he adds, "you will be limited by the level of your writing and performing. There is no one else on stage to push you and challenge you and make you look good. You are all alone, with your talent. Don't be discouraged but be realistic."

Every day, Precious delivered a new script with the date on it, often hot off Kinko's copy machine that morning. Some of the changes were minor, others encompassed reworked pages; in any case, we had to be on the same page as we kept building and shaping. Have I mentioned how much fun it was?

One day, her cell phone rang. We were technically on a break so she answered it. It was Wes, her fiancé, and I suddenly felt pangs of jealousy. My role in her life would inevitably shift with a marriage on the horizon. Our professional teaming had been a two-year-old marriage, with much of the intimacy and intensity of any marriage. If you haven't figured it out by now, I'm gay, so my primary interest in Precious was artistic. But how could it not go beyond that?

In many ways, and especially considering the amount of time we worked together, the director becomes father, brother, mother, sister, lover, confidant, therapist, stylist, cheerleader, critic, publicist, and friend. Being the type who wants to play all those roles to the hilt, I knew there had to be a shift. I also knew that it was appropriate, she deserved it, and I'd get over it.

By Friday, we brought Clinton in and worked the numbers, incorporating some costume changes that had to be retimed. I think this is when I had one of those light-bulb moments: the real shift of the piece was from the characters to Precious Chong. With the new material, especially the family prison scenes, the "old" characters, vivid as they were, couldn't compete. Even Porcelain Penelope began to fade by comparison. This would be another, and perhaps the biggest, challenge to face.

With the exception of the Sexy Mom character, Precious was less connected to the rest of her alter egos. While I thought that might work on some level, we still had to justify their existence. Time was at a premium and the hours were, at this juncture, needed to solve other, more immediate concerns. We could wait for Kim's input until after the first workshop performance.

The Mom monologues were getting trickier and trickier. Precious continued to paint her with humor but added a dimension of pathos that hadn't existed before. Shelby, along with Precious and Tommy, had been deeply affected by the many months of his imprisonment.

SEXY MOM

Prison changes you. I even go to the movies on my own now—every once in a while. I'm doing a TV show about me and Dad and I own it. Not Dad. Like Sharon Osbourne. In the beginning, in the beginning, it was hard not having Tommy around, being alone. I got too skinny. My tightest jeans actually looked loose on me. They hung on me. It's not good to be too skinny at my age. I'm much more political now. I mean, our country, our country is just so fucked up. The other night at Fran's birthday, Arianna Huffington was there with what's his name? You know the guy, you know, Precious. What's the guy I'm talking about? Oh, yeah, not Michael Moore, but the other one. Freckle? Freakle? Frankle? That's right! Al Franken! And I was just telling him about Tommy and he didn't even know about it. He's going to put it in his new book.

Yet another element of the Chong family's response to the patriarch being in jail was their quest for fame. I compare it to survivors of a loved one who become monsters in the process of getting the money and stuff they feel they deserve. It's some kind of solution to the pain. It's how the Chong family responded to the accelerated media attention.

If Papa Chong's career was resuscitated by doing time in the pokey, various family members (most of whom are in show biz) stood to benefit. Even Precious, who initially tried not to capitalize on her dad's imprisonment, wound up calling herself a "media whore." If the hoopla around Tommy was like a circus, there were family members who were eager to be in the sideshow. Remember the ballet? That former monologue was cut but the dance was rechoreographed to this new tale.

PRECIOUS

A Chong Family Christmas. My family is very Jane Austen. We go to other people's houses for a dinner. We exploit our circumstances. We go to Fran's for dinner. Fran is friends with Arianna Huffington. My mom goes on an angry rant. You see people's eyes glaze over. No one wants to see a pretty lady talk about politics. My dad performs a rap at the prison holiday party. He's OG: Old Gangster. My dad's ex-roommate sells his story to the *National Enquirer*. There are pictures of my dad gardening with other inmates. I'm quoted! Christmas day, my mom hides turkey in her boot to give to my dad. Steve Garbarino, the *Vanity Fair* writer, comes with us. I want him to like me. I'm a whore. A tabloid whore. *LA Weekly* does a story on my dad, but I tell the writer he can't interview my dad in person because of the *Vanity Fair* exclusive. The same weekend the article comes out, my dad is on the cover of *Valley Beat* with an exclusive in-person interview. I'm furious. "Precious, there's a reason Dad's in jail," my mom says. O'Reilly makes a glib comment about my father on Jay Leno. He's talking about my father and he's making stuff up. "The man's had eighteen previous convictions." He's defending Rush Limbaugh. He's a motherfucker. I write O'Reilly, Jay Leno, Warren Olney. I feel like Joan of Arc with e-mail.

She wore a white tutu with newspaper articles from the tabloids pinned on to it. We used Tchaikovsky's "Dance of the Sugar Plum Fairies" and Kim did a masterful job of making the movement merge with the words. And since we had more room at the Zephyr than we had at the Masquers, Kim was able to give her some dramatic twists and turns that supported the twists and turns in the writing.

"It was still a contrast or juxtaposition of stereotyped ballet in which everything is tight, specific, turned out, light, and idealized femininity, set against having your father in jail," Kim said. "But this version also used the ballet steps to express herself. Some of the steps went with, not against, the vehemence of her feelings, and her sense of self-righteousness. We used steps that exhibited strength and stamina—but, of course, in a ballet way."

We were still looking at more rewrites, so we opted to take Saturday off, push the tech to Monday, and do a final dress on Tuesday afternoon of the first workshop (June 8).

On Sunday, I had a brainstorm. Let's end the show with her wearing a wedding dress—something fluffy and lacy and over-the-top. After the innumerable costume changes signifying her former selves, she'd end up in a wedding dress, foreshadowing her future self.

This idea probably came from a memory of the first Broadway show I saw when I was a teenager: Angela Lansbury in *Mame*. At the end of the show, we knew she was going to marry Beauregard, but what a surprise when she came on for her curtain call in a wedding dress that was fully half the size of the stage at the Winter Garden.

One has to earn a costume. When I asked Precious to elaborate on her relationship with Wes, this is what she wrote:

PRECIOUS

What I don't tell my dad is that six days after Wes and I first kissed, I would've dropped everything to be with him, that he sings songs to me late at night with the prettiest, gentlest voice and then in the next moment orders me around in bed ("Keep your panties on"), that he proposed to me on my birthday and then every day after that, that he enacted the final scene of the first *Rocky* movie naked and playing all the parts, and that it's big love. Big, big love.

After the Sunday rehearsal, we decided to run to Goodwill and look at wedding dresses. Of all the memories I have of our many escapades, this was the best. It was Lucy and Ethel (or maybe Jane and Lily). It was madcap.

We arrived at the Goodwill and there were, indeed, several dresses to choose from. The gown needed to easily fit over her street clothing since the change would be somewhat fast and in front of the audience (unlike Angela's unexpected appearance). So our choices were limited.

We found one that was pretty great but not perfect. We were having a great time carrying on and people, especially the employees, were keeping an eye on us. Did they think we were getting married? That would have probably made more sense than the real story.

Precious spotted a dress that was still in what appeared to be its original box. A note on the price tag said, "Don't open." Huh?

"Are you saying that she can't try on the dress?" I politely ask the clerk.

"Yes," she says, adamantly.

"What? I can't try it on? You've got to be kidding," Precious says, joining the drama at the check-out area. She is getting shrill. "Is there a manager?"

"I'll call her," the poor clerk says. She picks up a telephone.

Now I'm getting shrill. "There's no manager *here in the store* who can authorize trying this on? Tell me something, would you buy a Goodwill wedding dress for $75 that you hadn't tried on?"

She laughs and nervously dials the phone.

"This is too much," Precious says as we go from laughing our heads off to acting like we're Sharon Stone and Jackie Collins at Saks Fifth Avenue.

We hear her explaining the situation on the phone. After what seems like an eternity, she hangs up and says, "No."

"She said no?" Precious and I shriek in unison.

Now there's a crowd gathered, including a middle-aged black man who takes our side and begins arguing. I'm convinced that he is a romantic and wants the bride and groom to be happy.

"They are right," he says. "Who would pay for a wedding dress without trying it on?"

Meanwhile, Precious is rummaging through her purse, looking for her credit card. They must think that I'm a cheap bastard, letting my wife-to-be buy her own wedding dress.

"Yah," I say, "Who would pay for a wedding dress without trying it on?" Beat. "I guess we would."

Precious hands the rattled clerk her card. She's laughing one minute and making sounds of exasperation the next. Once the sale is complete, we head for the dressing room. The black man follows us, along with several other people in the store who probably think this is a reality show being filmed.

The veil itself is about twenty feet long. Fabulous. And the dress is to die for, with a train that goes on for days. Precious puts it on amidst a chorus of "oohs" and "aahs" while the black man zips her up.

"You don't need to zip it, but thanks," I say. "She won't have it on for long." I cannot imagine what they thought I meant by that.

Precious and I were thrilled. We stuffed it back in the box and headed to the parking lot, exhausted.

"That black man thought we were gonna get married," I said.

She looked at me like I was nuts. "Are you kidding?" she said. "He was flirting with you."

"Really?" I said. "Maybe we should go back in there and get me a dress."

The Monday tech at the Zephyr with Gary went very well even though, as usual, it was longer and more tedious than we expected. We rehearsed with the dress, which would hang on the set with the other costumes, throughout the show.

Remember that moment at the top of the show when Precious, during her last visit to the prison, tries to tell her dad something? I needed to figure out a way to let the audience know that we were re-creating that moment at the end of the show. The wedding veil!

"Dad, I've got something to tell you," she says, and then whips on the ornate veil. At the top of the show, it got a big laugh and also teased the marriage. At the conclusion of the show, we had an obvious physical action to let us know that we had returned to that moment.

The first Tuesday night audience was relatively small and we were thankful for that. But they provided us with a game plan, based on what we could see was working and what needed clarifying. Our faithful supporter, Jenny, was there and once again suggested that we put Mr. H on tape so that Precious would have more time and energy to make the additional emotional adjustments required in this version.

Mr. H's lines, if added together, probably amounted to less than three or four minutes in length. As the show's emcee, he introduced each of the acts. With these introductions on tape, the audience was able to see Precious more fully become the character she was about to perform without the distraction of having her do Hitler's voice live.

Kim was there and expressed her concern about the dances. I agreed with her; they weren't working. What used to be the most flamboyant aspect of the show and the most entertaining had become the least exciting. "When I saw the show," Kim remembers,

> I used the word "confused" to describe my reaction. I did not like the dance numbers in the show, but wasn't sure why. I also remember thinking that the show had changed to accommodate the Masquers as a venue, as well as the developments in Precious' life, and now we were back to the venue where we had originated the show. It was sort of like coming home and realizing you had changed, and seeing it more clearly because now you were home again. I wasn't sure what the show was about at this point, and how the old pieces fit into the new show. Also, the music didn't seem to work as well as it had before.

To Kim the show seemed like "a third- or fourth-generation copy of something, where things get fuzzier rather than clearer—a less precise approximation." She felt that the numbers "had moved further away from their original source or intention. I wanted to go back to the music we had used to create the choreography, and I wanted to remember our original intention."

Kim had worked with Clinton only briefly and I, admittedly not a musician, had let things get sloppy. "Going back to the original recorded music," Kim said, "and working with Clinton, we were able to clean up some of the musical transitions, simplify some things, and refine others so that the musical accompaniment supported Precious much better. The accents and transitions had gotten messy, and were part of the muddy impression I had seeing the show that first night." This was the very essence of collaboration. Collaboration that required stamina for all three of us to make these changes happen.

In addition to the work on the dance numbers, Precious went into the recording studio to put Mr. H's lines on tape. At that point, we had to commit to those lines, since more recording would be costly and time-consuming. The biggest task I gave myself was to make the distinctions between the locations (onstage, backstage, the car, the prison) so that the emotional crescendos would resonate.

The second Tuesday went well. The dances were alive again, Jenny had been right about putting Mr. H on tape, and I felt that Precious was exploring the real meat of the show in a way that would have it flying by the time we got to New York. I spent a great deal of time during the show, as I always do, watching the faces of the audience to see how the show is affecting them. Respectfully, I avoided spending too much time looking at Shelby.

When a show is this far along, I'd rather give notes after a performance. In fact, I usually leave with the audience and call Precious' answering service. On that night, I told her how beautifully I thought things had gone. The next day, I received a disturbing message from Precious. It seemed that her mother was not happy with the new script and became hysterical only moments after the audience had left the theatre. I was in a tech rehearsal for another production but managed to get Precious on the phone directly.

"We had this screaming fight, right on the stage," Precious said. "She felt like I was making fun of her. She felt like it was mean. She said

101

she always feels like she's the joke. It was horrible. We were screaming and yelling at each other. You probably could have heard us on the street."

I was afraid that this incident might make her rethink the show and threaten the integrity of the brilliant work she'd accomplished. I wasn't about to get into that at this juncture, but I did assure her that I knew, if anyone knew, that it was not her intent to hurt her mother. In fact, the opposite was true: she had gone to great lengths to humanize the mother's role. But I also couldn't discount how her mother felt, and I thought we should consider putting that into the show as well.

"I'll be okay," she assured me. And she would.

She needed time. When I spoke to her again the next morning, she had begun processing it and so had Shelby. Precious was certain that her mother wouldn't see the show again and was concerned that she might convince her dad not to see it.

"In many ways, as painful as it is," I said, "this all makes sense. It's your show; it's your material. You own it. It does not belong to them even though they are a part of it."

"You know what line she really hates?" Precious asked.

"I can't imagine," I said. And I couldn't.

"'No dance class,'" she said. "I'll cut it."

On their way to see Tommy in jail, Shelby tells Precious that she's packed dance clothes so they would have something to look forward to after their visit. But when Tommy excuses himself to go to the bathroom, after insisting they stay longer, Shelby sadly realizes, "No dance class." It got a big laugh but Precious did cut it—the only three words she cut after the altercation with her mom.

There were, however, additions. Exactly one week after their blow-up, literally on the same stage, Precious gave her mother a chance to voice her position.

Sexy Mom

I'm not telling her one more thing because she just takes every little thing I say and puts it in her show. She's just like her dad. You know what? I'm tired of being the idiot out here. I mean, hasn't this been enough, this year? I just can't take one more thing, not one more thing. I have been with Tommy since I was seventeen years old. Seventeen, Precious. Do you know what that's like? Do you? You need to just grow up, do you hear me, just grow up. All of you. I am just tired of being the butt of everyone's joke. No more. I've had it. I've just had it. No, it's okay, honey. I just needed to get that out. I'm fine now. I'm fine. It's okay. I love you. I'm fine. I just need beautiful things around me—flowers, candles, creme de la mer. I'm happy for her. She met someone—a big handsome Canadian guy. He looks like one of Forrest's kids, my sister. Looks like someone from our family. I'm so happy for her. But just wait till she has kids. He doesn't have any money, but that's okay. She'll do really well in Toronto. But she needs to give the show a new title. I hate this freaky Penelope. But she doesn't listen to me. She's stubborn, like her dad. She needs to understand I'm not that type of mother. And why did Rain Pryor get the better dates? She needs to keep listening to those tapes I gave her. Those self-help tapes. "Excuse me your life is waiting." Honey, don't you want to get better? I do, I want to get better.

This was great work and she acted it with all her—and her mother's—heart. At one point, she cracks but pulls herself together. We placed Mom's rebuttal after the "Chong Family Christmas" ballet and before the last prison visit. One of the greatest lessons here is that, as a storyteller, it's often imperative to let the other person tell their side of the story. It's generous and fair—and can make terrific drama.

I had to leave town for the final workshop performance but it's always a good idea for the performer to have a break from the director. It had to be a relief not to have me in the audience, scribbling on my yellow pad.

I had previously planned a trip to my hometown of St. Louis with my daughter, and Precious, after the final workshop, packed up her apartment and moved to Canada. We began communicating online. There were some annoying e-mails that went back and forth between the theatre in New York, Precious, and me. Most of them had to do with their obsession with trying to bring Tommy into the loop. At one point, they actually asked if they could put his name on the promotional postcard, saying that he'd be attending the opening night.

"Do they know what the show is about?" I asked Precious, exasperated.

He had been released from jail and was living in a halfway house but was unable to get away to see any of the workshop performances. Whether any of her family members would be at the New York opening remained unanswered.

But there was no question that Wes, her betrothed, would be in the opening night audience to share her success. And there's no question that success and stamina are related.

Exercise/Stamina

Remember your collaborator? Time to meet again and rework all of your material. This will probably be your longest session (at least an hour or two) because you'll now see that you've got a piece in the making. But you need the stamina to do the work.

There are discoveries to be made. And rewrites to be done. And the physicalization of the words. And possibly making the adjustment from autobiography to fiction. And getting comfortable with the acting of your material.

This is also where you must remember that adage, "Don't let the truth get in the way of a good story." There may be something missing in what you've written that is needed to tie it all together. Make it up.

Or you may want to change one of the characters from a friend to your father for more impact. Be my guest. And maybe that black turtleneck would play better in the hospital scene than that retro red Hawaiian shirt.

You're almost there! And you've strengthened your stamina muscle. Congratulations.

Chapter 6 Checklist

- Do you have the stamina to wear both hats—as writer and performer?

- Are you able to assess your strengths and weaknesses as a writer and a performer and seek training if necessary?

- Do you have the stamina to rehearse for several hours and then rewrite for several more?

- Do you have the stamina to tour (if you're so lucky)?

- Do you have the stamina to be onstage for an hour?

- Do you have the stamina required to face rejection?

- Consider letting other characters you depict speak from their point of view even if it contradicts yours.

- Do you have the stamina necessary to do endless rewrites?

- Are you able to summon the stamina to go onstage, on your own, without the support of other cast members?

7 Success

Be willing to accept that there can be no failure—only abandonment.

Mark Travis

It was not the success story I'd written in my head. Precious and I met at the theatre on the Friday morning before the Sunday night performance. We went to the offices of Off-Off Broadway's Culture Project at 45 Bleecker, which were several flights up on an elevator that had a New York feel—dangerous, exciting, bumpy, and loud.

There were a few hip-looking young women scurrying about a typically messy office space. Precious politely introduced me. Alan Buchman, the artistic director, was shuffling through papers on his desk.

"Alan?" Precious said, "I'd like you to meet my director, Michael Kearns."

He must have grunted a response but he did not look up from his important papers. I never saw him or spoke to him again even though I assume he was at the opening night.

On the way down the elevator, Precious speculated that maybe they were disappointed because her dad couldn't be there on Sunday night. He had just been released to a halfway house in LA and they wouldn't allow him to leave town.

"Stop," I said. "Fuck 'em. That has never been part of the equation."

The tech guys were far more considerate despite the usual delays and inevitable rescheduling dramas. The game plan was arduous. The opening night performance would be set up for a party crowd, seated at tables. On Monday night, the theatre would be completely reconfigured. This meant two tech rehearsals and extensive restaging between the Sunday and Monday shows.

Although I can't speak for Precious, I didn't feel we were a success—not yet, anyway. But I don't even know what that would have felt like. What did I expect?

There's the key word: expect. We had worked harder on this version than on any of the others, partly because it was the most developed, but also because it was going to New York. Serious New York, not shallow Hollywood. Respected Off-Broadway, not crappy television and recycled movies. New York—hotbed of intellectual and artistic accomplishment, not derivative and predictable product without a heartbeat.

My expectations were based on the mythology that true success as an artist was nonexistent in LA. You could only claim success as a theatre person if you proved yourself in New York. Following this self-defeating train of thought, what would the Big Apple success story look like? A rave in the *New York Times*? An audience with Mike Nichols and Diane Sawyer in the front row? An invitation to do the *David Letterman Show*?

How one measures success varies and is often loaded with contradictions. One person's idea of success could be interpreted by another as utter failure. Or vice versa. This is particularly true in labeling an artistic venture as either a success or a failure. What aspect of success is being evaluated? Is the work an artistic success? A personal success? A professional success? A financial success? A spiritual success?

I stopped myself, knowing what I was doing was irrational. Solo performance has always been a primarily artistic venture for me. Making money, gaining unanimous approval from the masses, having consistently full houses, and being awarded for your work with movie roles is no longer part of the equation.

David Nichols believes that "success in performance has nothing to do with good reviews or monetary gain or positive feedback. It's about the degree to which artists feel safe to create what they must, for the sake of doing so."

As a writer-performer, my first show had its ups and downs but was unquestionably a personal triumph. A decade later, my second one-person show, *intimacies*, was a hit by anyone's standards. Two more smashes followed, *more intimacies* and *Rock*. These three shows, produced all over the world from 1989 to 1994, marked what might be referred to as the pinnacle of my success.

Subsequent solo shows (*Attachments, Tell Tale Kisses*) did not achieve the ostensible high regard that was given to the earlier three. It was, at times, difficult for me to reconcile. Was it over? Was I suddenly a failure? Where were the newspaper interviews? The full houses? The offers to tour?

In order to continue functioning as an artist, I had to be very clear about what success meant to me, and where I had control. I had no control over shifting media obsessions, the sexiness of gay issues and HIV/AIDS, or the audience's fickleness. What I did have control over were the stories I wanted to tell—stories of outcasts and misfits, of the disenfranchised and often diseased. My work was solid, well produced, carefully directed. I had something to say and the energy to get it from the stage to the audience.

My buddy Tim Miller once said, "My hope in my performances is that anytime we witness one person raise his voice and tell his story— as well as bring our focus to systems of injustice—it can encourage the rest to find that truth-telling place within ourselves. I have received that encouragement in my life from other theatre artists and social movements and I hope my performances have emboldened people as well. This is the success that truly matters."

If I gauge my success in terms of externals, maybe subsequent work has been less successful. But if I looked at my internal process, growth, and evolution, I am succeeding. Continuing to work with less ostensible encouragement and acceptance is, in itself, a sign of success.

Success is personal, based on the goals you have set. Keep in mind that one of the realities of solo is that you are a bit of a renegade. You break rules. Defy the so-called standards of success. Create and commit to your own standards and do not depend on the validation of others.

That said, the fact that Tommy was going to be on Friday's *Tonight Show* with Jay Leno seemed like monumental success was on the way. Precious hoped he would mention—or is the word plug?—her New York performances.

I could hardly stay awake to watch as I realized the absurdity of the situation. There I was, in my New York City hotel room, watching Tommy Chong, recently released from prison, talking to Jay Leno in Los Angeles, and hoping he'd talk about his daughter's Off-Off Broadway show so that millions of listeners would know (and thousands would try to purchase tickets).

Well, he didn't mention it. Talk about providing more perspective.

Back at work the next day, Precious and I barely mentioned it. We had work to do. She had sent all the costumes and props in advance. The most cumbersome item was the sign, made with small red and pink individual bulbs that spelled out P-O-R-C-E-L-A-I-N on a half moon piece of deliberately flimsy cardboard. Tacky and bedraggled, it was an accurate representation of the exhausted and loud child star.

Where to hang the sign was one of many decisions that had to be made on Saturday, in preparation of the relatively short four-hour tech on Sunday. Among other things, we were dealing with a raised stage that did not appear to be entirely safe, with uneven steps that Precious needed to be very confident negotiating.

The nightclub ambience was more like the Masquers and we were able to approximate the Zephyr's playing area to a degree, so we borrowed from both venues to make the new venue work (at least for the Sunday performance).

The room was much longer and we took advantage of that by bringing Snake Girl and (especially) Emma farther into the audience. We had a follow spot, which streamlined the lighting in many instances.

Thank God the technicians were efficient on Sunday, although typically they were doing several shows and didn't seem really invested in any of them.

If there was heightened attention being paid to anyone at the Culture Project it was, understandably, Sarah Jones. Produced in association with

Meryl Streep, Jones' *Bridge & Tunnel* was the current example of solo at its most successful. The upstairs lobby (which I suppose we technically shared with *Bridge & Tunnel*) was plastered with photos and newspaper articles that heaped lavish praise on Jones' solo turn. At one point, I chuckled to myself, We are beneath her—down in the basement. We are still underground; she's mainstream. There was truth in this, but so what? There was no comparison. Precious Chong and Sarah Jones have about as much in common as Tommy Chong and Jack Jones. They were merely sharing the same space.

I've always emphasized to my students that comparing one work to another is a destructive act. And nowhere is this truer than in solo. It is individual, not to be compared. Compare sitcoms, compare productions of Shakespeare, compare Williams to Inge, but it's virtually impossible to compare solo works because they are unique. Even if there appear to be similarities because the work is written and performed by the same person and possibly autobiographical in nature, it would be very hard to find two shows that were similar in execution and theme.

"Don't compare yourself to any other solo performer or show," Mark Travis insists. "It will make you either vain or bitter. That's their show, let them have it. Don't compete with it. Don't steal from it. Learn from their experience and do your own."

Precious and I had been through so many tech rehearsals that this one didn't seem much more stressful, although she seemed uncharacteristically cranky. It may have been because of the lack of support from the artistic director. It also could have been because she was feeling split between Wes, who was with us at the tech, and the show. He was an angel—bright, sweet, helpful, and totally interested in things other than himself (a contradiction considering his occupation).

The opening night was festive, with audience members in the mood to have a good time. Precious didn't disappoint. From the opening moment until the final "love letter" to Wes, she took the audience on a thrilling ride. I am constantly amazed at how people immediately fall in love with her. Her energy touches everyone in the room. She is vulnerable without trying to be—that's the key.

Seated at my table were Wes; Tom Viola, the executive director of Broadway Care/Equity Fights AIDS; Zo Harris, one of my newest friends, who came with me from LA; and Caroline Kava, a brilliant artist who has been a friend for nearly forty years. They were all very taken with the show, and I was proud of the success that I shared with Precious.

The next day, it was raining and we had to meet early to restage, relight, and reconfigure the entire show. We did it with as much energy as we could muster, even though it was not easy. We moved as quickly as we could and went over a few notes from the night before (nothing major) leaving us a few hours to nap before the second New York show.

There were only about a dozen people in the audience on that rainy Monday night. My concern was for Precious, but I knew she'd deal with it and wouldn't allow it to affect her work. I visited her dressing room. She was in that transitional mode I'd seen many times—somewhere between the offstage Precious and the onstage Precious. Her hair and makeup were done and the glow was beginning to appear.

The performance was truly inspired. I studied the responses of everyone in the house—laughing and crying; appreciating the irony, the darkness, the silliness, and the pain—all the ingredients that make Precious Chong and *The Porcelain Penelope Freak Show* such a success. She hit every note. Every moment was clean and clear and expertly executed. Without a trace of self-consciousness, she performed gracefully and truthfully, telling her story.

This was success, quiet success. Happy ending.

P.S. Precious and Wes were married before the end of the week.

Exercise/Success

If you did all of the exercises outlined in Chapters 1 through 6, you are a success! You took the journey and invested your time and energy and pulled something together, which is more than what 90 percent of the people out there who say they are going to do a one-person show actually accomplish.

I do not care about the result. I do not care if your neighbor thinks you're better than Anna Deveare Smith. I do not care if you think it's a piece of crap. I don't even care if you threw it away. It's not the outcome that determines success; it's not the applause or the reviews or the money or the fame. It's the artistic process.

If you want to be a soloist, you have to commit to being an artist. As I said, if you followed those simple exercises, you were in an artistic pursuit and that makes you a success. Again, congratulations. Keep writing. Keep emoting. Keep working.

Chapter 7 Checklist

- Are you willing to fail (maybe several times) before you succeed?
- Are you willing to define success in your own terms?
- Does an intrinsic fear of success prevent you from succeeding?
- Are you willing to do the work that's required to succeed?
- Are you trying to succeed in order to please other people?
- Do you have unrealistic expectations of what success looks like or feels like?
- Are you able to avoid making comparisons that threaten your potential success?
- Would a negative review make you unsuccessful?
- Do you think a solo show will make you rich and famous?
- Do you think of a solo show as a step to achieve mainstream success?

Conclusion

I have told you the story of Precious Chong's solo journey and how it moved back and forth, from the page to the stage, again and again, over the course of two years. Why? Because I want to inspire those who are considering a solo career to take the leap. I also want to warn you that it is not an easy road. I tried to amuse you on occasion as well as teach you a thing or two. I also wanted to let you know how much I love and respect the form.

I have great respect for Richard Boleslavsky's *Acting: The First Six Lessons* (Routledge, 1987), and I hope my homage to his beautiful book is taken as it is intended—a bit cheeky but with wholehearted admiration. *Acting: The First Six Lessons* should be required reading for any artist, and especially for soloists in the making.

If you think about it, this book's structure is not unlike that of a solo show. It too is like a train ride. In *The Solo Performer's Journey*, one has to stop at many stations (in this case, they are chapters) in order to arrive at the final destination, a finished book. In a solo work, you move from moment to moment or scene to scene or monologue to monologue (or some combination of those) as you tell your story. In a book you move from sentence to sentence, paragraph to paragraph, trying to put your story in an order that is both clear and entertaining and that's headed for a destination.

I've tried to condense all that happened in Precious' show's evolution—from our first meeting in LA in the summer of 2002 to the New York performance of *The Porcelain Penelope Freak Show*—spanning two years and separated by a couple of thousand miles. We hit some bumps along the way, other times we coasted, we encountered unexpected twists and turns followed by smooth sailing, sometimes we sped, and there were times it felt like we were flying.

What has been reconfirmed for me as a result of writing this book is the power that comes from telling your story, and the ownership of self that results. I have once again been energized by the galvanizing relationship between performer and audience in a live setting. And perhaps most exciting of all, I got in touch all over again with the gratitude I feel for having discovered solo work and having made it one of my primary means of artistic expression.

During the two-year unraveling of Precious Chong's saga, my daughter, Tia, began taking acting very seriously, giving my friends an opportunity to tease, "One day, there will be a one-person show about daddy Michael."

If Tia accomplishes a solo piece, with the passion and precision that Precious brought to the beautiful story of a father and daughter who love each other deeply, I'm ready. Bring it on.